THE TERRITORY NORTHWEST OF THE RIVER OHIO, PETITIONERS, ETC., 1790-1800 [1785-1804]

(Present day Indiana)
(1790 begins at page 4)

(1800 begins at page 22)

**BIBLIOGRAPHY FOR THE TERRITORY NORTHWEST OF THE RIVER OHIO,
PETITIONERS, ETC., 1790-1800 [1785-1804]**
(Present day Indiana)

United States, Department of State, compiled and edited by Clarence Edwin Carter, *The Territorial Papers of the United States* Washington, D.C.: Government Printing Office, 1934-1962. 26 volumes. National Archives microfilm publications: M0721
  vol. 1. The Territorial Papers of the United States, General.
  vols. II & III The Territory Northwest of the River Ohio, 1787-1803.
  vol. IV The Territory South of the River Ohio, 1790-1796.
  vols. V & VI The Territory of Mississippi, 1798-1817.
  vols. VII & VIII The Territory of Indiana, 1800-1816.
  vol. IX The Territory of Orleans, 1803-1812.
  vols. X - XII The Territory of Michigan, 1805-1837.
  vols. XIII - XV The Territory of Louisiana-Missouri, 1803-1821.
  vols. XVI & XVII The Territory of Illinois, 1809-1818.
  vol. XVIII The Territory of Alabama, 1817-1819.
  vols. XIX - XXI The Territory of Arkansas, 1819-1836.
  vols. XXII - XXVI The Territory of Florida, 1821-1845.

[Please note: *Larger lists of names, such as petitions, etc., will be entered into the database. Names found in regular governmental/public transactions that contain no individual biographical details will not be extracted.*]

IN-01 THE TERRITORY NORTHWEST OF THE RIVER OHIO, PETITIONERS, ETC., 1790-1800 [1785-1804] (Present day Indiana). This book was compiled from *Territorial Papers of the United States.* 1790 contains 242 names found on petitions, etc., including a census of heads of household for Vincennes. 1800 only includes 76 names and so is not as valuable as 1790. The population of Indiana would have increased significantly between 1790 and 1800. This is still a very early time prior to Indiana becoming a state. Unfortunately, there is no 1790 or 1800 census existing to help track these people. Therefore, we must do what we can with what is available. That is why this new book is so helpful. It is even better in some respects than the census because it helps us understand some of the challenges they faced. It also makes possible the determination of other records that might be available for further research such as land grants. Even the names of some Native Americans are listed. Some additional biographical details may be included, plus possible relationships with other family members. For information on how to obtain this book search by the title or "Books by John Stemmons" at Amazon.com. This comes automatically with a paperback binding. It includes but is not limited to petitions regarding:

- Issues relating to land.
- Heads of families settled at Post Vincennes on or before 1783 and residents at this time [13 Jul 1790] who are entitled to donation lands.
- Issues relating to Native Americans.

- Inhabitants of Vincennes who migrated to Vincennes around 1786 and received land, but never obtained a deed.
- Appointments about military and local officers, etc.

INDEXES

Indexes are expensive to compile.
Which is why many books do not have them. Most that do just have a simple name index. A noteworthy exception is the *Territorial Papers of the United States* which gives some limited context as explained below.
Indexes are expensive but using modern technology we at Stemmons Publishing have included nearly all the context you may need. 100% context is probably not possible such as in a census that lists multiple neighbors. Search for entries of the same page in our book(s) or the original document if you require more information.

PUBLICATIONS FROM STEMMONS PUBLISHING

These following publications are not just traditional alphabetical lists of names, they include the context of information with each name!!

Why is that so important? Because many of the names in our books were obtained from various sources including South Carolina jury lists, the *Territorial Papers of the United States* (28 volumes each with its own index), petitions, tax lists, etc., and like most books with indexes common names require a lot of time to check each entry in the index. Can you imagine how many Smiths you would have to go through page-by-page for a compilation the size of *Territorial Papers of the United States*? Their indexes provide some context such as signing a petition. No explanation is given of what, when, or why the petition was made. Because we have included the context with each name, you can easily search all the Smiths, Taylors, Browns, Williams, etc., without all the drudgery! And since most of us have common surnames, we may need some help. Now, the originals of the South Carolina jury lists are housed in the South Carolina Department of Archives and History. Therefore, you may not have access to the originals. The way we index names means it is almost as good as being at the Archives yourself and doubly so since these documents are loose papers and do not have an original index. Our books provide an enhanced way of using *Territorial Papers of the United States* that the original compilers did not envision. So, if you have this collection, your obtaining our books compiled from those volumes will help your access to *Territorial Papers of the United States* even if you are not interested in our books about South Carolina jury lists. Now, that's what I call achieving the potential of a real index! It takes the bare skeleton of a name on a list and covers it with the flesh, hair, eyes, etc., of a human body. The names are more able to stand alone by themselves than is the case with a traditional index. We did not index subjects. *Territorial Papers of the United States* did.

Checking a name from our books and going to the page in *Territorial Papers of the United States* will show the list of names. Those listed next to the person of interest may be neighbors and relatives.

242 Names

Alare, Louis, Territory NW of Ohio River, Post Vincennes
     Alare, Louis, Male
Heads of families settled at Post Vincennes on or before 1783 and residents at this time [13 Jul 1790] who are entitled to donation lands.
Territorial Papers of US - volume: 2 page: 285
Andrez, Joseph, Territory NW of Ohio River, Post Vincennes
     Andrez, Joseph, Male
Heads of families settled at Post Vincennes on or before 1783 and residents at this time [13 Jul 1790] who are entitled to donation lands.
Territorial Papers of US - volume: 2 page: 285
Atchenewaugh, , Territory NW of Ohio River
     Atchenewaugh, , Male **Color:** Native Am
     "Weya Chief"
Articles of Agreement with the Wabash Indians, 14 Mar 1792.
Territorial Papers of US - volume: 2 page: 375
Awpaighchenecaugh, , Territory NW of Ohio River
     Awpaighchenecaugh, , Male **Color:** Native Am
     "Weya Chief"
Articles of Agreement with the Wabash Indians, 14 Mar 1792.
Territorial Papers of US - volume: 2 page: 375
Baillarjon, Nicolaus, Territory NW of Ohio River, Post Vincennes
     Baillarjon, Nicolaus, Male
Heads of families settled at Post Vincennes on or before 1783 and residents at this time [13 Jul 1790] who are entitled to donation lands.
Territorial Papers of US - volume: 2 page: 285
Baroy, Francois, Junr Territory NW of Ohio River, Post Vincennes
     Baroy, Francois, Junr Male

Heads of families settled at Post Vincennes on or before 1783 and residents at this time [13 Jul 1790] who are entitled to donation lands.
Territorial Papers of US - volume: 2 page: 285
Baroye, Francois, Senr Territory NW of Ohio River, Post Vincennes
     Baroye, Francois, Senr Male
Heads of families settled at Post Vincennes on or before 1783 and residents at this time [13 Jul 1790] who are entitled to donation lands.
Territorial Papers of US - volume: 2 page: 285
Basinet, Angelic, Territory NW of Ohio River, Post Vincennes
     Basinet, Angelic, Female
     Widow of Francois Basinet
Heads of families settled at Post Vincennes on or before 1783 and residents at this time [13 Jul 1790] who are entitled to donation lands.
Territorial Papers of US - volume: 2 page: 286
Baulon, Amable, Territory NW of Ohio River, Post Vincennes
     Baulon, Amable, Male
Heads of families settled at Post Vincennes on or before 1783 and residents at this time [13 Jul 1790] who are entitled to donation lands.
Territorial Papers of US - volume: 2 page: 285
Beatty, E, Territory NW of Ohio River Knox County, Vincennes
     Beatty, E, Male
     A witness to the agreement. "Capt 1. Reg. U. States"
Articles of Agreement with the Wabash Indians, 14 Mar 1792.
Territorial Papers of US - volume: 2 page: 375
Becker, B, Territory NW of Ohio River Knox County, Vincennes
     Becker, B, Male
Address to Colonel Josiah Harmar by American inhabitants of Post Vincennes dated 4 Aug 1787
Territorial Papers of US - volume: 2 page: 65

Bergand, Charles, Territory NW of Ohio River, Post Vincennes
        Bergand, Charles, Male
Heads of families settled at Post Vincennes on or before 1783 and residents at this time [13 Jul 1790] who are entitled to donation lands.
Territorial Papers of US - volume: 2 page: 285

Binette, John Baptiste, Territory NW of Ohio River, Post Vincennes
        Binette, John Baptiste, Male
Heads of families settled at Post Vincennes on or before 1783 and residents at this time [13 Jul 1790] who are entitled to donation lands.
Territorial Papers of US - volume: 2 page: 285

Bird, Ross, Territory NW of Ohio River
        Knox County, Vincennes
        Bird, Ross, Male
        A witness to the agreement. "Ensn 1. U. States Reg."
Articles of Agreement with the Wabash Indians, 14 Mar 1792.
Territorial Papers of US - volume: 2 page: 375

Bonneau, Charles, Territory NW of Ohio River, Post Vincennes
        Bonneau, Charles, Male
Heads of families settled at Post Vincennes on or before 1783 and residents at this time [13 Jul 1790] who are entitled to donation lands.
Territorial Papers of US - volume: 2 page: 285

Bordeleau, Antoinie, Senr Territory NW of Ohio River, Post Vincennes
        Bordeleau, Antoinie, Senr Male
Heads of families settled at Post Vincennes on or before 1783 and residents at this time [13 Jul 1790] who are entitled to donation lands.
Territorial Papers of US - volume: 2 page: 285

Bordeleau, Michel, Territory NW of Ohio River, Post Vincennes
        Bordeleau, Michel, Male
Heads of families settled at Post Vincennes on or before 1783 and residents at this time [13 Jul 1790] who are entitled to donation lands.
Territorial Papers of US - volume: 2 page: 285

Bosseron, F, Territory NW of Ohio River
        Knox County, Vincennes
        Bosseron, F, Male
        "Juge"
Letter, 23 Jul 1790, from Antoine Gamelin and others to acting Governor Sargent giving tribute to Major Hamtramck.

Territorial Papers of US - volume: 2 page: 292

Bosseron, Francois, Territory NW of Ohio River, Post Vincennes
        Bosseron, Francois, Male
Heads of families settled at Post Vincennes on or before 1783 and residents at this time [13 Jul 1790] who are entitled to donation lands.
Territorial Papers of US - volume: 2 page: 285

Bosseron, Francois, Maj. Territory NW of Ohio River, Post Vincennes
        Bosseron, Francois, Maj. Male
Letter to Winthrop Sargent 3 Jul 1790 from individuals explaining their granting lands within the district.
Territorial Papers of US - volume: 2 page: 283

Boucher, Vital, Territory NW of Ohio River, Post Vincennes
        Boucher, Vital, Male
Heads of families settled at Post Vincennes on or before 1783 and residents at this time [13 Jul 1790] who are entitled to donation lands.
Territorial Papers of US - volume: 2 page: 285

Boyer, Louis, Junr Territory NW of Ohio River, Post Vincennes
        Boyer, Louis, Junr Male
Heads of families settled at Post Vincennes on or before 1783 and residents at this time [13 Jul 1790] who are entitled to donation lands.
Territorial Papers of US - volume: 2 page: 285

Boyer, Marie, Territory NW of Ohio River, Post Vincennes
        Boyer, Marie, Female
        Widow of Louis Boyer
Heads of families settled at Post Vincennes on or before 1783 and residents at this time [13 Jul 1790] who are entitled to donation lands.
Territorial Papers of US - volume: 2 page: 285

Brouillet, Francois, Territory NW of Ohio River, Post Vincennes
        Brouillet, Francois, Male
Heads of families settled at Post Vincennes on or before 1783 and residents at this time [13 Jul 1790] who are entitled to donation lands.
Territorial Papers of US - volume: 2 page: 285

Brouillet, Louis, Territory NW of Ohio River, Post Vincennes
        Brouillet, Louis, Male
Heads of families settled at Post Vincennes on or before 1783 and residents at this time [13 Jul 1790] who are entitled to donation lands.

Territorial Papers of US - volume: 2 page: 285
Brouillet, Michel,   Territory NW of Ohio River, Post Vincennes
        Brouillet, Michel,   Male
Heads of families settled at Post Vincennes on or before 1783 and residents at this time [13 Jul 1790] who are entitled to donation lands.
Territorial Papers of US - volume: 2 page: 285
Buntin, Robert,   Territory NW of Ohio River   Knox County, Vincennes
        Buntin, Robert, Male
        ". . . an early American settler at Vincenneswas a surveyor and for a long period clerk of the courts of Knox County, Northwest Territory, and Indiana Territory"
Letter from Governor St. Clair to Secretary Sargent, 6 Jul 1790
Territorial Papers of US - volume: 2 page: 284
Cardinal, Jacque,   Territory NW of Ohio River, Post Vincennes
        Cardinal, Jacque,   Male
Heads of families settled at Post Vincennes on or before 1783 and residents at this time [13 Jul 1790] who are entitled to donation lands.
Territorial Papers of US - volume: 2 page: 285
Cardinal, John Baptiste,   Territory NW of Ohio River, Post Vincennes
        Cardinal, John Baptiste,   Male
Heads of families settled at Post Vincennes on or before 1783 and residents at this time [13 Jul 1790] who are entitled to donation lands.
Territorial Papers of US - volume: 2 page: 285
Cardinal, Marie,   Territory NW of Ohio River, Post Vincennes
        Cardinal, Marie,   Female
        Widow of Nicolaus Cardinal
Heads of families settled at Post Vincennes on or before 1783 and residents at this time [13 Jul 1790] who are entitled to donation lands.
Territorial Papers of US - volume: 2 page: 286
Carter, Moses,   Territory NW of Ohio River, Post Vincennes
        Carter, Moses, Male
Heads of families settled at Post Vincennes on or before 1783 and residents at this time [13 Jul 1790] who are entitled to donation lands.
Territorial Papers of US - volume: 2 page: 285
Cartier, Pierre, Senr   Territory NW of Ohio River, Post Vincennes
        Cartier, Pierre, Senr   Male

Heads of families settled at Post Vincennes on or before 1783 and residents at this time [13 Jul 1790] who are entitled to donation lands.
Territorial Papers of US - volume: 2 page: 285
Caty, Antoine, Territory NW of Ohio River, Post Vincennes
        Caty, Antoine, Male
Heads of families settled at Post Vincennes on or before 1783 and residents at this time [13 Jul 1790] who are entitled to donation lands.
Territorial Papers of US - volume: 2 page: 285
Chabot, Joseph,   Territory NW of Ohio River, Post Vincennes
        Chabot, Joseph,   Male
Heads of families settled at Post Vincennes on or before 1783 and residents at this time [13 Jul 1790] who are entitled to donation lands.
Territorial Papers of US - volume: 2 page: 285
Chacowaatagh, ,   Territory NW of Ohio River
        Chacowaatagh, ,   Male   **Color:** Native Am
        "Weya Chief"
Articles of Agreement with the Wabash Indians, 14 Mar 1792.
Territorial Papers of US - volume: 2 page: 375
Chapard, Nicholaus,   Territory NW of Ohio River, Post Vincennes
        Chapard, Nicholaus,   Male
Heads of families settled at Post Vincennes on or before 1783 and residents at this time [13 Jul 1790] who are entitled to donation lands.
Territorial Papers of US - volume: 2 page: 286
Charbonneau, Jacob, Territory NW of Ohio River, Post Vincennes
        Charbonneau, Jacob,   Male
Heads of families settled at Post Vincennes on or before 1783 and residents at this time [13 Jul 1790] who are entitled to donation lands.
Territorial Papers of US - volume: 2 page: 285
Charpentier, John,   Territory NW of Ohio River, Post Vincennes
        Charpentier, John,   Male
Heads of families settled at Post Vincennes on or before 1783 and residents at this time [13 Jul 1790] who are entitled to donation lands.
Territorial Papers of US - volume: 2 page: 285
Chartier, Joseph,   Territory NW of Ohio River, Post Vincennes
        Chartier, Joseph,   Male

Heads of families settled at Post Vincennes on or before 1783 and residents at this time [13 Jul 1790] who are entitled to donation lands.
Territorial Papers of US - volume: 2 page: 285
Checunememshaw, , Territory NW of Ohio River
Checunememshaw, , Male **Color:** Native Am
"Eel River Chief"
Articles of Agreement with the Wabash Indians, 14 Mar 1792.
Territorial Papers of US - volume: 2 page: 375
Coder, Francois, Territory NW of Ohio River, Post Vincennes
Coder, Francois, Male
Heads of families settled at Post Vincennes on or before 1783 and residents at this time [13 Jul 1790] who are entitled to donation lands.
Territorial Papers of US - volume: 2 page: 285
Coder, Louis, Territory NW of Ohio River, Post Vincennes
Coder, Louis, Male
Heads of families settled at Post Vincennes on or before 1783 and residents at this time [13 Jul 1790] who are entitled to donation lands.
Territorial Papers of US - volume: 2 page: 285
Coder, Susanna, Territory NW of Ohio River, Post Vincennes
Coder, Susanna, Female
Widow of Pierre Coder
Heads of families settled at Post Vincennes on or before 1783 and residents at this time [13 Jul 1790] who are entitled to donation lands.
Territorial Papers of US - volume: 2 page: 286
Compagnot, Francois, Territory NW of Ohio River, Post Vincennes
Compagnot, Francois, Male
Heads of families settled at Post Vincennes on or before 1783 and residents at this time [13 Jul 1790] who are entitled to donation lands.
Territorial Papers of US - volume: 2 page: 285
Contomaumgaugh, , Territory NW of Ohio River
Contomaumgaugh, , Male **Color:** Native Am
"Weya Chief"
Articles of Agreement with the Wabash Indians, 14 Mar 1792.
Territorial Papers of US - volume: 2 page: 375

Cornieyer, Pierre, Territory NW of Ohio River, Post Vincennes
Cornieyer, Pierre, Male
Heads of families settled at Post Vincennes on or before 1783 and residents at this time [13 Jul 1790] who are entitled to donation lands.
Territorial Papers of US - volume: 2 page: 285
Cott, Philip, Territory NW of Ohio River Knox County, Vincennes
Cott, Philip, Male
Petition, 7 Aug 1797, to Congress by inhabitants of Knox County, who migrated to Vincennes around 1786 and received land, but never obtained a deed.
Territorial Papers of US - volume: 2 page: 621
Cott, Philip, Territory NW of Ohio River Knox County, Vincennes
Cott, Philip, Male
Petition, 27 Dec 1797, to Congress by American inhabitants of Vincennes who migrated to Vincennes around 1786 and received land, but never obtained a deed.
Territorial Papers of US - volume: 2 page: 636
Dagenet, Francoise, Territory NW of Ohio River, Post Vincennes
Dagenet, Francoise, Female
Widow of Francoise Dagenet
Heads of families settled at Post Vincennes on or before 1783 and residents at this time [13 Jul 1790] who are entitled to donation lands.
Territorial Papers of US - volume: 2 page: 287
Daigneau, Pierre, Territory NW of Ohio River, Post Vincennes
Daigneau, Pierre, Male
Heads of families settled at Post Vincennes on or before 1783 and residents at this time [13 Jul 1790] who are entitled to donation lands.
Territorial Papers of US - volume: 2 page: 286
Danys, Antoine, Territory NW of Ohio River, Post Vincennes
Danys, Antoine, Male
Heads of families settled at Post Vincennes on or before 1783 and residents at this time [13 Jul 1790] who are entitled to donation lands.
Territorial Papers of US - volume: 2 page: 286
Danys, Honnorez, Territory NW of Ohio River, Post Vincennes
Danys, Honnorez, Male
Heads of families settled at Post Vincennes on or before 1783 and residents at this time [13 Jul 1790] who are entitled to donation lands.

Territorial Papers of US - volume: 2 page: 286
Daperon, Veronique, Territory NW of Ohio River, Post Vincennes
Daperon, Veronique, Female
Widow of Gilliome Daperon
Heads of families settled at Post Vincennes on or before 1783 and residents at this time [13 Jul 1790] who are entitled to donation lands.
Territorial Papers of US - volume: 2 page: 287
De Elaureier, John Baptiste, Territory NW of Ohio River, Post Vincennes
De Elaureier, John Baptiste, Male
Heads of families settled at Post Vincennes on or before 1783 and residents at this time [13 Jul 1790] who are entitled to donation lands.
Territorial Papers of US - volume: 2 page: 286
De Elaureier, Louis, Territory NW of Ohio River, Post Vincennes
De Elaureier, Louis, Male
Heads of families settled at Post Vincennes on or before 1783 and residents at this time [13 Jul 1790] who are entitled to donation lands.
Territorial Papers of US - volume: 2 page: 286
Decker, Dinah (widow), Territory NW of Ohio River   Knox County, Vincennes
Decker, Dinah (widow), Female
Petition, 27 Dec 1797, to Congress by American inhabitants of Vincennes who migrated to Vincennes around 1786 and received land, but never obtained a deed.
Territorial Papers of US - volume: 2 page: 636
Decker, Joseph, Territory NW of Ohio River   Knox County, Vincennes
Decker, Joseph, Male
Petition, 7 Aug 1797, to Congress by inhabitants of Knox County, who migrated to Vincennes around 1786 and received land, but never obtained a deed.
Territorial Papers of US - volume: 2 page: 621
Decker, Luke, Territory NW of Ohio River   Knox County, Vincennes
Decker, Luke, Male
Letter, 23 Jul 1790, from Antoine Gamelin and others to acting Governor Sargent giving tribute to Major Hamtramck.
Territorial Papers of US - volume: 2 page: 292
Decker, Moses, Territory NW of Ohio River   Knox County, Vincennes
Decker, Moses, Male

Petition, 7 Aug 1797, to Congress by inhabitants of Knox County, who migrated to Vincennes around 1786 and received land, but never obtained a deed.
Territorial Papers of US - volume: 2 page: 621
Decker, Moses, Territory NW of Ohio River   Knox County, Vincennes
Decker, Moses, Male
Address to Colonel Josiah Harmar by American inhabitants of Post Vincennes dated 4 Aug 1787
Territorial Papers of US - volume: 2 page: 65
Decker, Moses, Territory NW of Ohio River   Knox County, Vincennes
Decker, Moses, Male
Petition, 27 Dec 1797, to Congress by American inhabitants of Vincennes who migrated to Vincennes around 1786 and received land, but never obtained a deed.
Territorial Papers of US - volume: 2 page: 636
Decker, Tobias, Territory NW of Ohio River   Knox County, Vincennes
Decker, Tobias, Male
Petition, 7 Aug 1797, to Congress by inhabitants of Knox County, who migrated to Vincennes around 1786 and received land, but never obtained a deed.
Territorial Papers of US - volume: 2 page: 621
Deline, L E, Territory NW of Ohio River, Post Vincennes
Deline, L E, Male
Letter to Winthrop Sargent 3 Jul 1790 from individuals explaining their granting lands within the district.
Territorial Papers of US - volume: 2 page: 283
Deline, L E, Territory NW of Ohio River Knox County, Vincennes
Deline, L E, Male
Letter, 23 Jul 1790, from Antoine Gamelin and others to acting Governor Sargent giving tribute to Major Hamtramck.
Territorial Papers of US - volume: 2 page: 292
Delisle, Amable, Territory NW of Ohio River, Post Vincennes
Delisle, Amable, Male
Heads of families settled at Post Vincennes on or before 1783 and residents at this time [13 Jul 1790] who are entitled to donation lands.
Territorial Papers of US - volume: 2 page: 286
Delisle, Charles, Territory NW of Ohio River, Post Vincennes
Delisle, Charles, Male

Heads of families settled at Post Vincennes on or before 1783 and residents at this time [13 Jul 1790] who are entitled to donation lands.
Territorial Papers of US - volume: 2 page: 286
Denorgon, Marian,   Territory NW of Ohio River, Post Vincennes
        Denorgon, Marian,   Female
        Widow of Louis Denorgon
Heads of families settled at Post Vincennes on or before 1783 and residents at this time [13 Jul 1790] who are entitled to donation lands.
Territorial Papers of US - volume: 2 page: 287
Denorgon, Marie,   Territory NW of Ohio River, Post Vincennes
        Denorgon, Marie,   Female
        Widow of Toussaints Denorgon
Heads of families settled at Post Vincennes on or before 1783 and residents at this time [13 Jul 1790] who are entitled to donation lands.
Territorial Papers of US - volume: 2 page: 287
Denye, Jacque,   Territory NW of Ohio River, Post Vincennes
        Denye, Jacque, Male
Heads of families settled at Post Vincennes on or before 1783 and residents at this time [13 Jul 1790] who are entitled to donation lands.
Territorial Papers of US - volume: 2 page: 286
Derause, Francois,   Territory NW of Ohio River, Post Vincennes
        Derause, Francois,   Male
Heads of families settled at Post Vincennes on or before 1783 and residents at this time [13 Jul 1790] who are entitled to donation lands.
Territorial Papers of US - volume: 2 page: 286
Derogier, Bonnaventure,   Territory NW of Ohio River, Post Vincennes
        Derogier, Bonnaventure,   Male
Heads of families settled at Post Vincennes on or before 1783 and residents at this time [13 Jul 1790] who are entitled to donation lands.
Territorial Papers of US - volume: 2 page: 286
Dielle, Charles,   Territory NW of Ohio River, Post Vincennes
        Dielle, Charles, Male
Heads of families settled at Post Vincennes on or before 1783 and residents at this time [13 Jul 1790] who are entitled to donation lands.
Territorial Papers of US - volume: 2 page: 286
Ditard, Nicolaus,   Territory NW of Ohio River, Post Vincennes

Ditard, Nicolaus,   Male
Heads of families settled at Post Vincennes on or before 1783 and residents at this time [13 Jul 1790] who are entitled to donation lands.
Territorial Papers of US - volume: 2 page: 286
Drouette, Antoine,   Territory NW of Ohio River, Post Vincennes
        Drouette, Antoine,   Male
Heads of families settled at Post Vincennes on or before 1783 and residents at this time [13 Jul 1790] who are entitled to donation lands.
Territorial Papers of US - volume: 2 page: 286
Dubois, John Baptiste,   Territory NW of Ohio River, Post Vincennes
        Dubois, John Baptiste, Male
Heads of families settled at Post Vincennes on or before 1783 and residents at this time [13 Jul 1790] who are entitled to donation lands.
Territorial Papers of US - volume: 2 page: 286
Ducharme, Joseph,   Territory NW of Ohio River, Post Vincennes
        Ducharme, Joseph,   Male
Heads of families settled at Post Vincennes on or before 1783 and residents at this time [13 Jul 1790] who are entitled to donation lands.
Territorial Papers of US - volume: 2 page: 286
Duchesne, John Baptiste,   Territory NW of Ohio River, Post Vincennes
        Duchesne, John Baptiste,   Male
Heads of families settled at Post Vincennes on or before 1783 and residents at this time [13 Jul 1790] who are entitled to donation lands.
Territorial Papers of US - volume: 2 page: 286
Dudevoir, Charles,   Territory NW of Ohio River, Post Vincennes
        Dudevoir, Charles,   Male
Heads of families settled at Post Vincennes on or before 1783 and residents at this time [13 Jul 1790] who are entitled to donation lands.
Territorial Papers of US - volume: 2 page: 286
Dumay, Agate,   Territory NW of Ohio River, Post Vincennes
        Dumay, Agate, Female
        Widow of Amable Dumay
Heads of families settled at Post Vincennes on or before 1783 and residents at this time [13 Jul 1790] who are entitled to donation lands.
Territorial Papers of US - volume: 2 page: 287
Edeline, Louis,   Territory NW of Ohio River, Post Vincennes

Edeline, Louis, Male
Heads of families settled at Post Vincennes on or before 1783 and residents at this time [13 Jul 1790] who are entitled to donation lands.
Territorial Papers of US - volume: 2 page: 286
et Andrez Racine, Pierre,   Territory NW of Ohio River, Post Vincennes
et Andrez Racine, Pierre,   Male
Heads of families settled at Post Vincennes on or before 1783 and residents at this time [13 Jul 1790] who are entitled to donation lands.
Territorial Papers of US - volume: 2 page: 286
Flamelin, Joseph,   Territory NW of Ohio River, Post Vincennes
Flamelin, Joseph,   Male
Heads of families settled at Post Vincennes on or before 1783 and residents at this time [13 Jul 1790] who are entitled to donation lands.
Territorial Papers of US - volume: 2 page: 286
Frederick, Sabastian, Territory NW of Ohio River   Knox County, Vincennes
Frederick, Sabastian,   Male
Petition, 27 Dec 1797, to Congress by American inhabitants of Vincennes who migrated to Vincennes around 1786 and received land, but never obtained a deed.
Territorial Papers of US - volume: 2 page: 636
Fredric, Sebastian,   Territory NW of Ohio River   Knox County, Vincennes
Fredric, Sebastian,   Male
Petition, 7 Aug 1797, to Congress by inhabitants of Knox County, who migrated to Vincennes around 1786 and received land, but never obtained a deed.
Territorial Papers of US - volume: 2 page: 621
Fredric, Widow Mary,   Territory NW of Ohio River   Knox County, Vincennes
Fredric, Widow Mary,   Female
Petition, 7 Aug 1797, to Congress by inhabitants of Knox County, who migrated to Vincennes around 1786 and received land, but never obtained a deed.
Territorial Papers of US - volume: 2 page: 621
Fredrick, Louis,   Territory NW of Ohio River   Knox County, Vincennes
Fredrick, Louis,   Male
Petition, 27 Dec 1797, to Congress by American inhabitants of Vincennes who migrated to Vincennes around 1786 and received land, but never obtained a deed.
Territorial Papers of US - volume: 2 page: 636

Fredrick, Louis,   Territory NW of Ohio River   Knox County, Vincennes
Fredrick, Louis,   Male
Petition, 7 Aug 1797, to Congress by inhabitants of Knox County, who migrated to Vincennes around 1786 and received land, but never obtained a deed.
Territorial Papers of US - volume: 2 page: 621
Fredrick, Mary (widow),   Territory NW of Ohio River   Knox County, Vincennes
Fredrick, Mary (widow),   Female
Petition, 27 Dec 1797, to Congress by American inhabitants of Vincennes who migrated to Vincennes around 1786 and received land, but never obtained a deed.
Territorial Papers of US - volume: 2 page: 636
Fredrick, Peter,   Territory NW of Ohio River   Knox County, Vincennes
Fredrick, Peter, Male
Petition, 27 Dec 1797, to Congress by American inhabitants of Vincennes who migrated to Vincennes around 1786 and received land, but never obtained a deed.
Territorial Papers of US - volume: 2 page: 636
Gallionois, Alexis Astruse,   Territory NW of Ohio River, Post Vincennes
Gallionois, Alexis Astruse,   Male
Heads of families settled at Post Vincennes on or before 1783 and residents at this time [13 Jul 1790] who are entitled to donation lands.
Territorial Papers of US - volume: 2 page: 286
Gamelin, Antoine,   Territory NW of Ohio River   Knox County, Vincennes
Gamelin, Antoine,   Male
"Juge quarter Cession"
Letter, 23 Jul 1790, from Antoine Gamelin and others to acting Governor Sargent giving tribute to Major Hamtramck.
Territorial Papers of US - volume: 2 page: 292
Gamelin, Antoine,   Territory NW of Ohio River, Post Vincennes
Gamelin, Antoine,   Male
Heads of families settled at Post Vincennes on or before 1783 and residents at this time [13 Jul 1790] who are entitled to donation lands.
Territorial Papers of US - volume: 2 page: 286
Gamelin, Antonie,   Territory NW of Ohio River   Knox County, Vincennes
Gamelin, Antonie,   Male   **Job:** Secretary & Greffier

Petition, July 26, 1787 on behalf of inhabitants of Post Vincennes for 520000 acres
Territorial Papers of US - volume: 2 page: 60
Gamelin, Paul,   Territory NW of Ohio River, Post Vincennes
          Gamelin, Paul, Male
Heads of families settled at Post Vincennes on or before 1783 and residents at this time [13 Jul 1790] who are entitled to donation lands.
Territorial Papers of US - volume: 2 page: 286
Gamelin, Paul,   Territory NW of Ohio River   Knox County, Vincennes
          Gamelin, Paul, Male
          "Juge"
Letter, 23 Jul 1790, from Antoine Gamelin and others to acting Governor Sargent giving tribute to Major Hamtramck.
Territorial Papers of US - volume: 2 page: 292
Gamelin, Pierre,   Territory NW of Ohio River   Knox County, Vincennes
          Gamelin, Pierre,   Male **Job:** Magistrate
Petition, July 26, 1787 on behalf of inhabitants of Post Vincennes for 520000 acres
Territorial Papers of US - volume: 2 page: 60
Gamelin, Pierre,   Territory NW of Ohio River, Post Vincennes
          Gamelin, Pierre,   Male
Heads of families settled at Post Vincennes on or before 1783 and residents at this time [13 Jul 1790] who are entitled to donation lands.
Territorial Papers of US - volume: 2 page: 286
Gamelin, Pierre,   Territory NW of Ohio River   Knox County, Vincennes
          Gamelin, Pierre,   Male
          "Juge"
Letter, 23 Jul 1790, from Antoine Gamelin and others to acting Governor Sargent giving tribute to Major Hamtramck.
Territorial Papers of US - volume: 2 page: 292
Gamelin, Pierre,   Territory NW of Ohio River, Post Vincennes
          Gamelin, Pierre,   Male
          "Appointed Judge of Court of Common Pleas, Indiana Territory, Aug. 3, 1801"
Letter to Winthrop Sargent 3 Jul 1790 from individuals explaining their granting lands within the district.
Territorial Papers of US - volume: 2 page: 283

Gaurguipis, Amable,   Territory NW of Ohio River, Post Vincennes
          Gaurguipis, Amable,   Male
Heads of families settled at Post Vincennes on or before 1783 and residents at this time [13 Jul 1790] who are entitled to donation lands.
Territorial Papers of US - volume: 2 page: 286
Gilbert, Pierre,   Territory NW of Ohio River, Post Vincennes
          Gilbert, Pierre, Male
Heads of families settled at Post Vincennes on or before 1783 and residents at this time [13 Jul 1790] who are entitled to donation lands.
Territorial Papers of US - volume: 2 page: 286
Glass, Heirs of John,   Territory NW of Ohio River   Knox County, Vincennes
          Glass, Heirs of John,   Male
Petition, 27 Dec 1797, to Congress by American inhabitants of Vincennes who migrated to Vincennes around 1786 and received land, but never obtained a deed.
Territorial Papers of US - volume: 2 page: 636
Glass, Heirs of John,   Territory NW of Ohio River   Knox County, Vincennes
          Glass, Heirs of John,   Male
Petition, 7 Aug 1797, to Congress by inhabitants of Knox County, who migrated to Vincennes around 1786 and received land, but never obtained a deed.
Territorial Papers of US - volume: 2 page: 621
Goder, Tousaint,   Territory NW of Ohio River, Post Vincennes
          Goder, Tousaint,   Male
Heads of families settled at Post Vincennes on or before 1783 and residents at this time [13 Jul 1790] who are entitled to donation lands.
Territorial Papers of US - volume: 2 page: 286
Godere dit Pannah, Renez,   Territory NW of Ohio River, Post Vincennes
          Godere dit Pannah, Renez,   Male
Heads of families settled at Post Vincennes on or before 1783 and residents at this time [13 Jul 1790] who are entitled to donation lands.
Territorial Papers of US - volume: 2 page: 287
Grimare, Gennevieve, Territory NW of Ohio River, Post Vincennes
          Grimare, Gennevieve, Female
          Widow of Pierre Grimare
Heads of families settled at Post Vincennes on or before 1783 and residents at this time [13 Jul 1790] who are entitled to donation lands.

Territorial Papers of US - volume: 2 page: 287
Guielle, Charles,   Territory NW of Ohio River, Post Vincennes
          Guielle, Charles,   Male
Heads of families settled at Post Vincennes on or before 1783 and residents at this time [13 Jul 1790] who are entitled to donation lands.
Territorial Papers of US - volume: 2 page: 286
H[a]rbin, Eliz (widow),   Territory NW of Ohio River   Knox County, Vincennes
          H[a]rbin, Eliz (widow), Female
Petition, 7 Aug 1797, to Congress by inhabitants of Knox County, who migrated to Vincennes around 1786 and received land, but never obtained a deed.
Territorial Papers of US - volume: 2 page: 621
Hamtramack, , Major Territory NW of Ohio River, Vincennes
          Hamtramack, , Major   Male
          He is "the Commandant at Post St Vincennes"
Mentioned in letter, 13 Dec 1788, from Governor St. Clair to the Secretary for Foreign Affairs [pages 166-170].
Territorial Papers of US - volume: 2 page: 170
Hamtramck, John Francis,   Territory NW of Ohio River   Knox County, Vincennes
          Hamtramck, John Francis,   Male
          "Major of the 1st United States Regimt"
Articles of Agreement with the Wabash Indians, 14 Mar 1792.
Territorial Papers of US - volume: 2 page: 374
Harmar, Josiah, Colonel   Territory NW of Ohio River   Knox County, Vincennes
          Harmar, Josiah, Colonel Male
Address by American inhabitants of Post Vincennes dated 4 Aug 1787
Territorial Papers of US - volume: 2 page: 65
Harpin, John Baptiste,   Territory NW of Ohio River, Post Vincennes
          Harpin, John Baptiste,   Male
Heads of families settled at Post Vincennes on or before 1783 and residents at this time [13 Jul 1790] who are entitled to donation lands.
Territorial Papers of US - volume: 2 page: 286
Henry, Ann,   Territory NW of Ohio River, Post Vincennes
          Henry, Ann,   Female
          Widow of Moses Henry

Heads of families settled at Post Vincennes on or before 1783 and residents at this time [13 Jul 1790] who are entitled to donation lands.
Territorial Papers of US - volume: 2 page: 287
Hinton, Elizh (widow),   Territory NW of Ohio River   Knox County, Vincennes
          Hinton, Elizh (widow), Female
Petition, 27 Dec 1797, to Congress by American inhabitants of Vincennes who migrated to Vincennes around 1786 and received land, but never obtained a deed.
Territorial Papers of US - volume: 2 page: 636
Hinton, Elizth (Widow),   Territory NW of Ohio River   Knox County, Vincennes
          Hinton, Elizth (Widow),   Female
Petition, 7 Aug 1797, to Congress by inhabitants of Knox County, who migrated to Vincennes around 1786 and received land, but never obtained a deed.
Territorial Papers of US - volume: 2 page: 621
Holeday, Jas, Territory NW of Ohio River   Knox County, Vincennes
          Holeday, Jas,   Male
Address to Colonel Josiah Harmar by American inhabitants of Post Vincennes dated 4 Aug 1787
Territorial Papers of US - volume: 2 page: 65
Holliday, Heirs of James,   Territory NW of Ohio River   Knox County, Vincennes
          Holliday, Heirs of James,   Male
Petition, 7 Aug 1797, to Congress by inhabitants of Knox County, who migrated to Vincennes around 1786 and received land, but never obtained a deed.
Territorial Papers of US - volume: 2 page: 621
Holliday, Heirs of James,   Territory NW of Ohio River   Knox County, Vincennes
          Holliday, Heirs of James,   Male
Petition, 27 Dec 1797, to Congress by American inhabitants of Vincennes who migrated to Vincennes around 1786 and received land, but never obtained a deed.
Territorial Papers of US - volume: 2 page: 636
Hough, Chrisn,   Territory NW of Ohio River   Knox County, Vincennes
          Hough, Chrisn, Male
Petition, 27 Dec 1797, to Congress by American inhabitants of Vincennes who migrated to Vincennes around 1786 and received land, but never obtained a deed.
Territorial Papers of US - volume: 2 page: 636
Hunot, Joseph, Senr Territory NW of Ohio River, Post Vincennes

Hunot, Joseph, Senr   Male

Heads of families settled at Post Vincennes on or before 1783 and residents at this time [13 Jul 1790] who are entitled to donation lands.

Territorial Papers of US - volume: 2 page: 286

Jacques, Etienne, Territory NW of Ohio River, Post Vincennes

Jacques, Etienne,   Male

Heads of families settled at Post Vincennes on or before 1783 and residents at this time [13 Jul 1790] who are entitled to donation lands.

Territorial Papers of US - volume: 2 page: 286

Johnson, Jams, Territory NW of Ohio River   Knox County, Vincennes

Johnson, Jams,   Male

Petition, 27 Dec 1797, to Congress by American inhabitants of Vincennes who migrated to Vincennes around 1786 and received land, but never obtained a deed.

Territorial Papers of US - volume: 2 page: 636

Johnson, Jas, Territory NW of Ohio River   Knox County, Vincennes

Johnson, Jas,   Male

"Juge"

Letter, 23 Jul 1790, from Antoine Gamelin and others to acting Governor Sargent giving tribute to Major Hamtramck.

Territorial Papers of US - volume: 2 page: 292

Johnson, Jas, Territory NW of Ohio River   Knox County, Vincennes

Johnson, Jas,   Male

Address to Colonel Josiah Harmar by American inhabitants of Post Vincennes dated 4 Aug 1787

Territorial Papers of US - volume: 2 page: 65

Johnston, Edward, Territory NW of Ohio River, Post Vincennes

Johnston, Edward,   Male

Heads of families settled at Post Vincennes on or before 1783 and residents at this time [13 Jul 1790] who are entitled to donation lands.

Territorial Papers of US - volume: 2 page: 286

Johnston, Robert, Territory NW of Ohio River   Knox County, Vincennes

Johnston, Robert,   Male

Petition, 7 Aug 1797, to Congress by inhabitants of Knox County, who migrated to Vincennes around 1786 and received land, but never obtained a deed.

Territorial Papers of US - volume: 2 page: 621

Johnston, Robert, Territory NW of Ohio River   Knox County, Vincennes

Johnston, Robert,   Male

Petition, 27 Dec 1797, to Congress by American inhabitants of Vincennes who migrated to Vincennes around 1786 and received land, but never obtained a deed.

Territorial Papers of US - volume: 2 page: 636

Johnston, Washington, Territory NW of Ohio River   Knox County, Vincennes

Johnston, Washington, Male   **Job:** Deputy Postmaster

"In 1783 emigrated from Virginia to Vincennesin which town he was the first attorney admitted to practice; subsequently circuit judge and legislator in the State of Indiana"

Appointed Deputy Postmaster of Vincennes "on a former occasion".

Territorial Papers of US - volume: 3 page: 78

Joyale, John Baptiste, Territory NW of Ohio River, Post Vincennes

Joyale, John Baptiste,   Male

Heads of families settled at Post Vincennes on or before 1783 and residents at this time [13 Jul 1790] who are entitled to donation lands.

Territorial Papers of US - volume: 2 page: 286

Kickapooquaigh, , Territory NW of Ohio River

Kickapooquaigh, ,   Male   **Color:** Native Am

Weya Chief

Articles of Agreement with the Wabash Indians, 14 Mar 1792.

Territorial Papers of US - volume: 2 page: 375

La Marc, Louis, Territory NW of Ohio River, Post Vincennes

La Marc, Louis,   Male

Heads of families settled at Post Vincennes on or before 1783 and residents at this time [13 Jul 1790] who are entitled to donation lands.

Territorial Papers of US - volume: 2 page: 286

La Poussiere, , Territory NW of Ohio River

La Poussiere, ,   Male   **Color:** Native Am

"Weya Chief"

Articles of Agreement with the Wabash Indians, 14 Mar 1792.

Territorial Papers of US - volume: 2 page: 375

Labuissiere, Gennevieve, Territory NW of Ohio River, Post Vincennes

Labuissiere, Gennevieve,   Female

Wife of Joseph Labuissiere--The Husband deserted.
Heads of families settled at Post Vincennes on or before 1783 and residents at this time [13 Jul 1790] who are entitled to donation lands.
Territorial Papers of US - volume: 2 page: 287
Lacroix, Jacque, Territory NW of Ohio River, Post Vincennes
Lacroix, Jacque, Male
Heads of families settled at Post Vincennes on or before 1783 and residents at this time [13 Jul 1790] who are entitled to donation lands.
Territorial Papers of US - volume: 2 page: 286
Laderoute, Louis, Territory NW of Ohio River, Post Vincennes
Laderoute, Louis, Male
Heads of families settled at Post Vincennes on or before 1783 and residents at this time [13 Jul 1790] who are entitled to donation lands.
Territorial Papers of US - volume: 2 page: 286
Lafontaine, Catarine, Territory NW of Ohio River, Post Vincennes
Lafontaine, Catarine, Female
Widow of John Baptiste Lafontaine
Heads of families settled at Post Vincennes on or before 1783 and residents at this time [13 Jul 1790] who are entitled to donation lands.
Territorial Papers of US - volume: 2 page: 287
Laforest, Pierre, Territory NW of Ohio River, Post Vincennes
Laforest, Pierre, Male
Heads of families settled at Post Vincennes on or before 1783 and residents at this time [13 Jul 1790] who are entitled to donation lands.
Territorial Papers of US - volume: 2 page: 286
Lagarde, Maudelin, Territory NW of Ohio River, Post Vincennes
Lagarde, Maudelin, Female
Widow of St Jean Lagarde
Heads of families settled at Post Vincennes on or before 1783 and residents at this time [13 Jul 1790] who are entitled to donation lands.
Territorial Papers of US - volume: 2 page: 287
Lamotte, Jacque, Territory NW of Ohio River, Post Vincennes
Lamotte, Jacque, Male
Heads of families settled at Post Vincennes on or before 1783 and residents at this time [13 Jul 1790] who are entitled to donation lands.
Territorial Papers of US - volume: 2 page: 286

Langlois, Renez, Territory NW of Ohio River, Post Vincennes
Langlois, Renez, Male
Heads of families settled at Post Vincennes on or before 1783 and residents at this time [13 Jul 1790] who are entitled to donation lands.
Territorial Papers of US - volume: 2 page: 286
Languedoc, Andrez, Territory NW of Ohio River, Post Vincennes
Languedoc, Andrez, Male
Heads of families settled at Post Vincennes on or before 1783 and residents at this time [13 Jul 1790] who are entitled to donation lands.
Territorial Papers of US - volume: 2 page: 286
Languedoc, Charles, Territory NW of Ohio River, Post Vincennes
Languedoc, Charles, Male
Heads of families settled at Post Vincennes on or before 1783 and residents at this time [13 Jul 1790] who are entitled to donation lands.
Territorial Papers of US - volume: 2 page: 286
Languedoc, Francois, Territory NW of Ohio River, Post Vincennes
Languedoc, Francois, Male
Heads of families settled at Post Vincennes on or before 1783 and residents at this time [13 Jul 1790] who are entitled to donation lands.
Territorial Papers of US - volume: 2 page: 286
Lardoise, Caterine, Territory NW of Ohio River, Post Vincennes
Lardoise, Caterine, Female
Widow of Amable Lardoise
Heads of families settled at Post Vincennes on or before 1783 and residents at this time [13 Jul 1790] who are entitled to donation lands.
Territorial Papers of US - volume: 2 page: 287
Latrimouille, Jacque, Territory NW of Ohio River, Post Vincennes
Latrimouille, Jacque, Male
Heads of families settled at Post Vincennes on or before 1783 and residents at this time [13 Jul 1790] who are entitled to donation lands.
Territorial Papers of US - volume: 2 page: 286
Leech, Geo, Territory NW of Ohio River Knox County, Vincennes
Leech, Geo, Male
Petition, 27 Dec 1797, to Congress by American inhabitants of Vincennes who migrated to Vincennes around 1786 and received land, but never obtained a deed.

Territorial Papers of US - volume: 2 page: 636
Leech, Geoe, Territory NW of Ohio River
     Knox County, Vincennes
     Leech, Geoe,   Male
Petition, 7 Aug 1797, to Congress by inhabitants of
Knox County, who migrated to Vincennes around
1786 and received land, but never obtained a deed.
Territorial Papers of US - volume: 2 page: 621
Lefevre, Louisa, Territory NW of Ohio
River, Post Vincennes
     Lefevre, Louisa,   Female
     Widow of Antoine Lefevre
Heads of families settled at Post Vincennes on or
before 1783 and residents at this time [13 Jul 1790]
who are entitled to donation lands.
Territorial Papers of US - volume: 2 page: 287
Legrace, J. M. P., Territory NW of Ohio
River   Knox County, Vincennes
     Legrace, J. M. P.,   Male   **Job:**
     First Magistrate
     "Col. J. M. P. Legras was a captain of
militia at Vincennes under the British and . . .
became a loyal subject of the [US & Virginia]. In
1779 he was appointed president of the Vincennes
court"
Name on petition, July 26, 1787 on behalf of
inhabitants of Post Vincennes for 520000 acres
Territorial Papers of US - volume: 2 page: 60
Legrand, Veronie, Territory NW of Ohio
River, Post Vincennes
     Legrand, Veronie,   Female
     Widow of Gabriel Legrand
Heads of families settled at Post Vincennes on or
before 1783 and residents at this time [13 Jul 1790]
who are entitled to donation lands.
Territorial Papers of US - volume: 2 page: 287
Legrass, Marie Louis, Territory NW of Ohio
River, Post Vincennes
     Legrass, Marie Louis,   Female
     Widow of John Phillip Marie Legrass
Heads of families settled at Post Vincennes on or
before 1783 and residents at this time [13 Jul 1790]
who are entitled to donation lands.
Territorial Papers of US - volume: 2 page: 287
Levens, Heirs of Widow, Territory NW of
Ohio River   Knox County, Vincennes
     Levens, Heirs of Widow,   Male
Petition, 7 Aug 1797, to Congress by inhabitants of
Knox County, who migrated to Vincennes around
1786 and received land, but never obtained a deed.

Territorial Papers of US - volume: 2 page: 621
Levrond, Joseph, Territory NW of Ohio
River, Post Vincennes
     Levrond, Joseph,   Male
Heads of families settled at Post Vincennes on or
before 1783 and residents at this time [13 Jul 1790]
who are entitled to donation lands.
Territorial Papers of US - volume: 2 page: 286
Lognon, Francois, Territory NW of Ohio
River, Post Vincennes
     Lognon, Francois,   Male
Heads of families settled at Post Vincennes on or
before 1783 and residents at this time [13 Jul 1790]
who are entitled to donation lands.
Territorial Papers of US - volume: 2 page: 286
Lognon, Joseph, Territory NW of Ohio
River, Post Vincennes
     Lognon, Joseph,   Male
Heads of families settled at Post Vincennes on or
before 1783 and residents at this time [13 Jul 1790]
who are entitled to donation lands.
Territorial Papers of US - volume: 2 page: 286
Luneford, Antony, Territory NW of Ohio
River, Post Vincennes
     Luneford, Antony,   Male
Heads of families settled at Post Vincennes on or
before 1783 and residents at this time [13 Jul 1790]
who are entitled to donation lands.
Territorial Papers of US - volume: 2 page: 286
Mahl, Frederick, Territory NW of Ohio
River, Post Vincennes
     Mahl, Frederick,   Male
Heads of families settled at Post Vincennes on or
before 1783 and residents at this time [13 Jul 1790]
who are entitled to donation lands.
Territorial Papers of US - volume: 2 page: 286
Mallet, Francois, Territory NW of Ohio
River, Post Vincennes
     Mallet, Francois,   Male
Heads of families settled at Post Vincennes on or
before 1783 and residents at this time [13 Jul 1790]
who are entitled to donation lands.
Territorial Papers of US - volume: 2 page: 286
Mallette, Antonie, Territory NW of Ohio
River, Post Vincennes
     Mallette, Antonie,   Male
Heads of families settled at Post Vincennes on or
before 1783 and residents at this time [13 Jul 1790]
who are entitled to donation lands.
Territorial Papers of US - volume: 2 page: 286

Mallette, Joseph, Territory NW of Ohio River, Post Vincennes
Mallette, Joseph, Male
Heads of families settled at Post Vincennes on or before 1783 and residents at this time [13 Jul 1790] who are entitled to donation lands.
Territorial Papers of US - volume: 2 page: 286
Mallette, Pierre, Territory NW of Ohio River, Post Vincennes
Mallette, Pierre, Male
Heads of families settled at Post Vincennes on or before 1783 and residents at this time [13 Jul 1790] who are entitled to donation lands.
Territorial Papers of US - volume: 2 page: 286
Mangen, John Baptiste, Territory NW of Ohio River, Post Vincennes
Mangen, John Baptiste, Male
Heads of families settled at Post Vincennes on or before 1783 and residents at this time [13 Jul 1790] who are entitled to donation lands.
Territorial Papers of US - volume: 2 page: 286
Marier, Antonie, Territory NW of Ohio River, Post Vincennes
Marier, Antonie, Male
Heads of families settled at Post Vincennes on or before 1783 and residents at this time [13 Jul 1790] who are entitled to donation lands.
Territorial Papers of US - volume: 2 page: 286
Martin, John, Territory NW of Ohio River Knox County, Vincennes
Martin, John, Male
Petition, 7 Aug 1797, to Congress by inhabitants of Knox County, who migrated to Vincennes around 1786 and received land, but never obtained a deed.
Territorial Papers of US - volume: 2 page: 621
Martin, John, Territory NW of Ohio River Knox County, Vincennes
Martin, John, Male
Petition, 27 Dec 1797, to Congress by American inhabitants of Vincennes who migrated to Vincennes around 1786 and received land, but never obtained a deed.
Territorial Papers of US - volume: 2 page: 636
Matson, Ralph, Territory NW of Ohio River Knox County, Vincennes
Matson, Ralph, Male
Petition, 27 Dec 1797, to Congress by American inhabitants of Vincennes who migrated to Vincennes around 1786 and received land, but never obtained a deed.

Territorial Papers of US - volume: 2 page: 636
Matson, Ralph, Territory NW of Ohio River Knox County, Vincennes
Matson, Ralph, Male
Petition, 7 Aug 1797, to Congress by inhabitants of Knox County, who migrated to Vincennes around 1786 and received land, but never obtained a deed.
Territorial Papers of US - volume: 2 page: 621
Mayes, Robt, Territory NW of Ohio River Knox County, Vincennes
Mayes, Robt, Male
Petition, 27 Dec 1797, to Congress by American inhabitants of Vincennes who migrated to Vincennes around 1786 and received land, but never obtained a deed.
Territorial Papers of US - volume: 2 page: 636
Mayot, Nicolaus, Territory NW of Ohio River, Post Vincennes
Mayot, Nicolaus, Male
Heads of families settled at Post Vincennes on or before 1783 and residents at this time [13 Jul 1790] who are entitled to donation lands.
Territorial Papers of US - volume: 2 page: 286
Mehl, Fredk, Territory NW of Ohio River Knox County, Vincennes
Mehl, Fredk, Male
Petition, 27 Dec 1797, to Congress by American inhabitants of Vincennes who migrated to Vincennes around 1786 and received land, but never obtained a deed.
Territorial Papers of US - volume: 2 page: 636
Meteyer, Louis, Territory NW of Ohio River, Post Vincennes
Meteyer, Louis, Male
Heads of families settled at Post Vincennes on or before 1783 and residents at this time [13 Jul 1790] who are entitled to donation lands.
Territorial Papers of US - volume: 2 page: 286
Milliet, John Baptiste, Territory NW of Ohio River, Post Vincennes
Milliet, John Baptiste, Male
Heads of families settled at Post Vincennes on or before 1783 and residents at this time [13 Jul 1790] who are entitled to donation lands.
Territorial Papers of US - volume: 2 page: 286
Minie, Francois, Territory NW of Ohio River, Post Vincennes
Minie, Francois, Male
Heads of families settled at Post Vincennes on or

before 1783 and residents at this time [13 Jul 1790] who are entitled to donation lands.
Territorial Papers of US - volume: 2 page: 286
Mitchel, Joseph, Territory NW of Ohio River, Post Vincennes
Mitchel, Joseph, Male
Heads of families settled at Post Vincennes on or before 1783 and residents at this time [13 Jul 1790] who are entitled to donation lands.
Territorial Papers of US - volume: 2 page: 286
Mois, John Baptiste, Territory NW of Ohio River, Post Vincennes
Mois, John Baptiste, Male
Heads of families settled at Post Vincennes on or before 1783 and residents at this time [13 Jul 1790] who are entitled to donation lands.
Territorial Papers of US - volume: 2 page: 286
Monplesir, Andrez, Territory NW of Ohio River, Post Vincennes
Monplesir, Andrez, Male
Heads of families settled at Post Vincennes on or before 1783 and residents at this time [13 Jul 1790] who are entitled to donation lands.
Territorial Papers of US - volume: 2 page: 286
Morgan, , Territory NW of Ohio River
Morgan, , Male
Mentioned in letter, 1 May 1790, from Cahokia by Governor St. Clair to the President [pages 244-248].
[page 247] "In a Letter, which I had the honor to address to you from the Rapids of Ohio, I mentioned the Information I had received respecting Mr Morgan in that part of the Country.--I found that he had been still busier here, if possible: in order to induce the Inhabitants to abandon the Country and follow him, he had a number of Sacks of Earth brought up from the Ance de la Graise [New Madrid], to shew them, and convince them of its very superior Quality; but his chief Argument, and that which operated most powerfully, was drawn from that Article in the Constitution of the Territory which respects Slaves--he assured them, most positively, that they would all be liberated without any Compensation being made to the owners--He pressed them to save them while it was yet in their Power--that the Governor was then on his way, and after his arrival it would be too late--to fly if they had any regard to themselves--they had not a moment to lose:--it had the Effect to drive away many respectable

Inhabitants, but not the Effect he expected, very few followed him, but they took refuge on the opposite Shore and became Subjects of Spain, which they now very heartily regret--He is now at this Moment sending away the Inhabitants of New Jersey to that Country under printed Passports directed to all civil and military Officers and requiring them to receive them as Subjects of his Catholic Majesty."
Territorial Papers of US - volume: 2 page: 247
Murphy, John, Territory NW of Ohio River Knox County, Vincennes
Murphy, John, Male
Petition, 27 Dec 1797, to Congress by American inhabitants of Vincennes who migrated to Vincennes around 1786 and received land, but never obtained a deed.
Territorial Papers of US - volume: 2 page: 636
Neau, Michael, Territory NW of Ohio River, Post Vincennes
Neau, Michael, Male
Heads of families settled at Post Vincennes on or before 1783 and residents at this time [13 Jul 1790] who are entitled to donation lands.
Territorial Papers of US - volume: 2 page: 286
Noy, Mary (widow), Territory NW of Ohio River Knox County, Vincennes
Noy, Mary (widow), Female
Petition, 27 Dec 1797, to Congress by American inhabitants of Vincennes who migrated to Vincennes around 1786 and received land, but never obtained a deed.
Territorial Papers of US - volume: 2 page: 636
Noy, Widow Mary, Territory NW of Ohio River Knox County, Vincennes
Noy, Widow Mary, Female
Petition, 7 Aug 1797, to Congress by inhabitants of Knox County, who migrated to Vincennes around 1786 and received land, but never obtained a deed.
Territorial Papers of US - volume: 2 page: 621
Ouilette, John Baptiste, Territory NW of Ohio River, Post Vincennes
Ouilette, John Baptiste, Male
Heads of families settled at Post Vincennes on or before 1783 and residents at this time [13 Jul 1790] who are entitled to donation lands.
Territorial Papers of US - volume: 2 page: 286
Pancake, Widow Mary, Territory NW of Ohio River Knox County, Vincennes
Pancake, Widow Mary, Female

Petition, 7 Aug 1797, to Congress by inhabitants of Knox County, who migrated to Vincennes around 1786 and received land, but never obtained a deed.
Territorial Papers of US - volume: 2 page: 621
Pannah dit Godere, Renez, Territory NW of Ohio River, Post Vincennes
Pannah dit Godere, Renez, Male
Heads of families settled at Post Vincennes on or before 1783 and residents at this time [13 Jul 1790] who are entitled to donation lands.
Territorial Papers of US - volume: 2 page: 287
Panncake, Mary (widow), Territory NW of Ohio River Knox County, Vincennes
Panncake, Mary (widow), Female
Petition, 27 Dec 1797, to Congress by American inhabitants of Vincennes who migrated to Vincennes around 1786 and received land, but never obtained a deed.
Territorial Papers of US - volume: 2 page: 636
Payes, Guillaume, Territory NW of Ohio River, Post Vincennes
Payes, Guillaume, Male
Heads of families settled at Post Vincennes on or before 1783 and residents at this time [13 Jul 1790] who are entitled to donation lands.
Territorial Papers of US - volume: 2 page: 286
Pea, Rachel (widow), Territory NW of Ohio River Knox County, Vincennes
Pea, Rachel (widow), Female
Petition, 27 Dec 1797, to Congress by American inhabitants of Vincennes who migrated to Vincennes around 1786 and received land, but never obtained a deed.
Territorial Papers of US - volume: 2 page: 636
Pea, Widow Rachel, Territory NW of Ohio River Knox County, Vincennes
Pea, Widow Rachel, Female
Petition, 7 Aug 1797, to Congress by inhabitants of Knox County, who migrated to Vincennes around 1786 and received land, but never obtained a deed.
Territorial Papers of US - volume: 2 page: 621
Peankeunshaw, , Territory NW of Ohio River
Peankeunshaw, , Male **Color:** Native Am
"Eel River Chief"
Articles of Agreement with the Wabash Indians, 14 Mar 1792.
Territorial Papers of US - volume: 2 page: 375

Perodeau, Joseph, Territory NW of Ohio River, Post Vincennes
Perodeau, Joseph, Male
Heads of families settled at Post Vincennes on or before 1783 and residents at this time [13 Jul 1790] who are entitled to donation lands.
Territorial Papers of US - volume: 2 page: 286
Perret, Pierre, Territory NW of Ohio River, Post Vincennes
Perret, Pierre, Male
Heads of families settled at Post Vincennes on or before 1783 and residents at this time [13 Jul 1790] who are entitled to donation lands.
Territorial Papers of US - volume: 2 page: 286
Perron, Amable, Territory NW of Ohio River, Post Vincennes
Perron, Amable, Male
Heads of families settled at Post Vincennes on or before 1783 and residents at this time [13 Jul 1790] who are entitled to donation lands.
Territorial Papers of US - volume: 2 page: 286
Perrot, Mary Louis, Territory NW of Ohio River, Post Vincennes
Perrot, Mary Louis, Female
Widow of Nicholaus Perrot
Heads of families settled at Post Vincennes on or before 1783 and residents at this time [13 Jul 1790] who are entitled to donation lands.
Territorial Papers of US - volume: 2 page: 286
Perrot, N., Territory NW of Ohio River Knox County, Vincennes
Perrot, N., Male **Job:** Magistrate
Petition, July 26, 1787 on behalf of inhabitants of Post Vincennes for 520000 acres
Territorial Papers of US - volume: 2 page: 60
Pettier, Felicitie, Territory NW of Ohio River, Post Vincennes
Pettier, Felicitie, Female
Widow of Francois Pettier
Heads of families settled at Post Vincennes on or before 1783 and residents at this time [13 Jul 1790] who are entitled to donation lands.
Territorial Papers of US - volume: 2 page: 286
Pettier, Louisa, Territory NW of Ohio River, Post Vincennes
Pettier, Louisa, Female
Widow of Andre Pettier
Heads of families settled at Post Vincennes on or

before 1783 and residents at this time [13 Jul 1790] who are entitled to donation lands.
Territorial Papers of US - volume: 2 page: 286

Phillibert, Angelic, Territory NW of Ohio River, Post Vincennes
Phillibert, Angelic, Female
Widow of Ettienne Phillibert
Heads of families settled at Post Vincennes on or before 1783 and residents at this time [13 Jul 1790] who are entitled to donation lands.
Territorial Papers of US - volume: 2 page: 286

Prior, A, Territory NW of Ohio River Knox County, Vincennes
Prior, A, Male
A witness to the agreement. "Lt 1. U. States Regt"
Articles of Agreement with the Wabash Indians, 14 Mar 1792.
Territorial Papers of US - volume: 2 page: 375

Pullaaswaigh, , Territory NW of Ohio River
Pullaaswaigh, , Male **Color:** Native Am
"Weya Chief"
Articles of Agreement with the Wabash Indians, 14 Mar 1792.
Territorial Papers of US - volume: 2 page: 375

Quenez, Pierre, Senr Territory NW of Ohio River, Post Vincennes
Quenez, Pierre, Senr Male
Heads of families settled at Post Vincennes on or before 1783 and residents at this time [13 Jul 1790] who are entitled to donation lands.
Territorial Papers of US - volume: 2 page: 286

Querez, Pierre, Territory NW of Ohio River, Post Vincennes
Querez, Pierre, Male
He signed his name with an "x"
Letter to Winthrop Sargent 3 Jul 1790 from individuals explaining their granting lands within the district.
Territorial Papers of US - volume: 2 page: 283

Racine, Francois, Territory NW of Ohio River, Post Vincennes
Racine, Francois, Male
Heads of families settled at Post Vincennes on or before 1783 and residents at this time [13 Jul 1790] who are entitled to donation lands.
Territorial Papers of US - volume: 2 page: 286

Ramsey, Allen, Territory NW of Ohio River Knox County, Vincennes
Ramsey, Allen, Male
Petition, 7 Aug 1797, to Congress by inhabitants of Knox County, who migrated to Vincennes around 1786 and received land, but never obtained a deed.
Territorial Papers of US - volume: 2 page: 621

Raux, Joseph, Territory NW of Ohio River, Post Vincennes
Raux, Joseph, Male
Heads of families settled at Post Vincennes on or before 1783 and residents at this time [13 Jul 1790] who are entitled to donation lands.
Territorial Papers of US - volume: 2 page: 286

Ravalet, Louis, Territory NW of Ohio River, Post Vincennes
Ravalet, Louis, Male
Heads of families settled at Post Vincennes on or before 1783 and residents at this time [13 Jul 1790] who are entitled to donation lands.
Territorial Papers of US - volume: 2 page: 286

Rengez, Pierre, Territory NW of Ohio River, Post Vincennes
Rengez, Pierre, Male
Heads of families settled at Post Vincennes on or before 1783 and residents at this time [13 Jul 1790] who are entitled to donation lands.
Territorial Papers of US - volume: 2 page: 286

Robins, John, Territory NW of Ohio River Knox County, Vincennes
Robins, John, Male
Petition, 27 Dec 1797, to Congress by American inhabitants of Vincennes who migrated to Vincennes around 1786 and received land, but never obtained a deed.
Territorial Papers of US - volume: 2 page: 636

Robins, John, Territory NW of Ohio River Knox County, Vincennes
Robins, John, Male
Petition, 7 Aug 1797, to Congress by inhabitants of Knox County, who migrated to Vincennes around 1786 and received land, but never obtained a deed.
Territorial Papers of US - volume: 2 page: 621

Roussiault, Louis, Territory NW of Ohio River, Post Vincennes
Roussiault, Louis, Male
Heads of families settled at Post Vincennes on or before 1783 and residents at this time [13 Jul 1790] who are entitled to donation lands.
Territorial Papers of US - volume: 2 page: 286

Sabolle, Joseph, Territory NW of Ohio River, Post Vincennes
Sabolle, Joseph, Male
Heads of families settled at Post Vincennes on or before 1783 and residents at this time [13 Jul 1790] who are entitled to donation lands.
Territorial Papers of US - volume: 2 page: 286
Silby, Thomas, Territory NW of Ohio River   Knox County, Vincennes
Silby, Thomas, Male
Petition, 7 Aug 1797, to Congress by inhabitants of Knox County, who migrated to Vincennes around 1786 and received land, but never obtained a deed.
Territorial Papers of US - volume: 2 page: 621
Silby, Thos, Territory NW of Ohio River   Knox County, Vincennes
Silby, Thos, Male
Petition, 27 Dec 1797, to Congress by American inhabitants of Vincennes who migrated to Vincennes around 1786 and received land, but never obtained a deed.
Territorial Papers of US - volume: 2 page: 636
Small, Jno, Territory NW of Ohio River   Knox County, Vincennes
Small, Jno, Male
Address to Colonel Josiah Harmar by American inhabitants of Post Vincennes dated 4 Aug 1787
Territorial Papers of US - volume: 2 page: 65
St Aubin, John Baptiste, Territory NW of Ohio River, Post Vincennes
St Aubin, John Baptiste, Male
Heads of families settled at Post Vincennes on or before 1783 and residents at this time [13 Jul 1790] who are entitled to donation lands.
Territorial Papers of US - volume: 2 page: 286
St Marie Racine, John Baptiste, Territory NW of Ohio River, Post Vincennes
St Marie Racine, John Baptiste, Male
Heads of families settled at Post Vincennes on or before 1783 and residents at this time [13 Jul 1790] who are entitled to donation lands.
Territorial Papers of US - volume: 2 page: 286
St Marie, Etienne, Territory NW of Ohio River, Post Vincennes
St Marie, Etienne, Male
Heads of families settled at Post Vincennes on or before 1783 and residents at this time [13 Jul 1790] who are entitled to donation lands.
Territorial Papers of US - volume: 2 page: 286

St Marie, Joseph, Territory NW of Ohio River, Post Vincennes
St Marie, Joseph, Male
Heads of families settled at Post Vincennes on or before 1783 and residents at this time [13 Jul 1790] who are entitled to donation lands.
Territorial Papers of US - volume: 2 page: 286
Stone, Maudelin, Territory NW of Ohio River, Post Vincennes
Stone, Maudelin, Female
Widow of Joseph Stone
Heads of families settled at Post Vincennes on or before 1783 and residents at this time [13 Jul 1790] who are entitled to donation lands.
Territorial Papers of US - volume: 2 page: 287
Tardiveau, Barthelemi, Territory NW of Ohio River   Knox County, Vincennes
Tardiveau, Barthelemi, Male
Name on petition, 7 Aug 1787 on behalf of inhabitants of Post Vincennes for 520000 acres
Territorial Papers of US - volume: 2 page: 61
Tardiveau, Bartholomew, Territory NW of Ohio River   Knox County, Vincennes
Tardiveau, Bartholomew, Male
"A French mercantile adventurer. In 1793 he was attached to the Genet mission as interpreter."
Petition, 7 Aug 1787, to Congress from Post Vincennes by Bartholomew Tardiveau in behalf of the American inhabitants seeking for a grant of 500 acres for each male.
Territorial Papers of US - volume: 2 page: 67
Teverbough, Jacob, Territory NW of Ohio River   Knox County, Vincennes
Teverbough, Jacob, Male
Petition, 7 Aug 1797, to Congress by inhabitants of Knox County, who migrated to Vincennes around 1786 and received land, but never obtained a deed.
Territorial Papers of US - volume: 2 page: 621
Teverbough, Jacob, Territory NW of Ohio River   Knox County, Vincennes
Teverbough, Jacob, Male
Petition, 27 Dec 1797, to Congress by American inhabitants of Vincennes who migrated to Vincennes around 1786 and received land, but never obtained a deed.
Territorial Papers of US - volume: 2 page: 636
Thorn, Michael, Junr Territory NW of Ohio River   Knox County, Vincennes
Thorn, Michael, Junr Male

Petition, 27 Dec 1797, to Congress by American inhabitants of Vincennes who migrated to Vincennes around 1786 and received land, but never obtained a deed.
Territorial Papers of US - volume: 2 page: 636
Tougas, John Baptiste, Territory NW of Ohio River, Post Vincennes
Tougas, John Baptiste, Male
Heads of families settled at Post Vincennes on or before 1783 and residents at this time [13 Jul 1790] who are entitled to donation lands.
Territorial Papers of US - volume: 2 page: 286
Tougas, Joseph, Territory NW of Ohio River, Post Vincennes
Tougas, Joseph, Male
Heads of families settled at Post Vincennes on or before 1783 and residents at this time [13 Jul 1790] who are entitled to donation lands.
Territorial Papers of US - volume: 2 page: 286
Trudel, Francois, Territory NW of Ohio River, Post Vincennes
Trudel, Francois, Male
Heads of families settled at Post Vincennes on or before 1783 and residents at this time [13 Jul 1790] who are entitled to donation lands.
Territorial Papers of US - volume: 2 page: 286
Turpin, Francois, Territory NW of Ohio River, Post Vincennes
Turpin, Francois, Male
Heads of families settled at Post Vincennes on or before 1783 and residents at this time [13 Jul 1790] who are entitled to donation lands.
Territorial Papers of US - volume: 2 page: 286
Vachette, Francois, Territory NW of Ohio River, Post Vincennes
Vachette, Francois, Male
Heads of families settled at Post Vincennes on or before 1783 and residents at this time [13 Jul 1790] who are entitled to donation lands.
Territorial Papers of US - volume: 2 page: 286
Vallez, Alexander, Territory NW of Ohio River, Post Vincennes
Vallez, Alexander, Male
Heads of families settled at Post Vincennes on or before 1783 and residents at this time [13 Jul 1790] who are entitled to donation lands.
Territorial Papers of US - volume: 2 page: 286
Van Der Burgh, H, Territory NW of Ohio River   Knox County, Vincennes

Van Der Burgh, H, Male **Job:** "Major Militia"
Letter, 23 Jul 1790, from Antoine Gamelin and others to acting Governor Sargent giving tribute to Major Hamtramck.
Territorial Papers of US - volume: 2 page: 292
Vaudrye, Antonie, Territory NW of Ohio River, Post Vincennes
Vaudrye, Antonie, Male
Heads of families settled at Post Vincennes on or before 1783 and residents at this time [13 Jul 1790] who are entitled to donation lands.
Territorial Papers of US - volume: 2 page: 286
Vaudrye, John Baptiste, Territory NW of Ohio River, Post Vincennes
Vaudrye, John Baptiste, Male
Heads of families settled at Post Vincennes on or before 1783 and residents at this time [13 Jul 1790] who are entitled to donation lands.
Territorial Papers of US - volume: 2 page: 286
Vaudrye, John Baptiste, Junr Territory NW of Ohio River, Post Vincennes
Vaudrye, John Baptiste, Junr Male
Heads of families settled at Post Vincennes on or before 1783 and residents at this time [13 Jul 1790] who are entitled to donation lands.
Territorial Papers of US - volume: 2 page: 286
Vigo, F, Territory NW of Ohio River   Knox County, Vincennes
Vigo, F, Male **Job:** "Major des Milices"
Letter, 23 Jul 1790, from Antoine Gamelin and others to acting Governor Sargent giving tribute to Major Hamtramck.
Territorial Papers of US - volume: 2 page: 292
Vigo, Francois, Territory NW of Ohio River, Post Vincennes
Vigo, Francois, Male
Heads of families settled at Post Vincennes on or before 1783 and residents at this time [13 Jul 1790] who are entitled to donation lands.
Territorial Papers of US - volume: 2 page: 286
Vilray, John Baptiste, Territory NW of Ohio River, Post Vincennes
Vilray, John Baptiste, Male
Heads of families settled at Post Vincennes on or before 1783 and residents at this time [13 Jul 1790] who are entitled to donation lands.
Territorial Papers of US - volume: 2 page: 286

Westfall, Abram, Territory NW of Ohio River   Knox County, Vincennes
　　　　Westfall, Abram,　　Male
Petition, 27 Dec 1797, to Congress by American inhabitants of Vincennes who migrated to Vincennes around 1786 and received land, but never obtained a deed.
Territorial Papers of US - volume: 2 page: 636
Westfall, John, Territory NW of Ohio River   Knox County, Vincennes
　　　　Westfall, John,　Male
Petition, 7 Aug 1797, to Congress by inhabitants of Knox County, who migrated to Vincennes around 1786 and received land, but never obtained a deed.
Territorial Papers of US - volume: 2 page: 621
Westfall, John, Territory NW of Ohio River   Knox County, Vincennes
　　　　Westfall, John,　Male
Petition, 27 Dec 1797, to Congress by American inhabitants of Vincennes who migrated to Vincennes around 1786 and received land, but never obtained a deed.
Territorial Papers of US - volume: 2 page: 636
Willson, Ann (widow), Territory NW of Ohio River   Knox County, Vincennes

　　　　Willson, Ann (widow),　Female
Petition, 27 Dec 1797, to Congress by American inhabitants of Vincennes who migrated to Vincennes around 1786 and received land, but never obtained a deed.
Territorial Papers of US - volume: 2 page: 636
Willson, Widow Ann, Territory NW of Ohio River   Knox County, Vincennes
　　　　Willson, Widow Ann,　Female
Petition, 7 Aug 1797, to Congress by inhabitants of Knox County, who migrated to Vincennes around 1786 and received land, but never obtained a deed.
Territorial Papers of US - volume: 2 page: 621
Wilmore, John, Territory NW of Ohio River   Knox County, Vincennes
　　　　Wilmore, John,　Male
Petition, 27 Dec 1797, to Congress by American inhabitants of Vincennes who migrated to Vincennes around 1786 and received land, but never obtained a deed.
Territorial Papers of US - volume: 2 page: 636

THE TERRITORY NORTHWEST OF THE RIVER OHIO, PETITIONERS, ETC., 1800
[1795-1804]

76 Names

Bailey, John, Indiana Territory   Knox County
　　　　Bailey, John,　Male
Name on recommendation, 1804, by citizens of Knox County that General John Gibson be appointed Indian Agent.
Territorial Papers of the US - volume: 7 page: 251
Balshar, George, Indiana Territory   Knox County
　　　　Balshar, George,　Male
Name on recommendation, 1804, by citizens of Knox County that General John Gibson be appointed Indian Agent.
Territorial Papers of the US - volume: 7 page: 251
Barkman, Abm, Indiana Territory   Knox County

　　　　Barkman, Abm,　Male
Name on recommendation, 1804, by citizens of Knox County that General John Gibson be appointed Indian Agent.
Territorial Papers of the US - volume: 7 page: 251
Barkman, Henry, Indiana Territory   Knox County
　　　　Barkman, Henry,　Male
Name on recommendation, 1804, by citizens of Knox County that General John Gibson be appointed Indian Agent.
Territorial Papers of the US - volume: 7 page: 251
Barron, Joseph, Indiana Territory   Knox County
　　　　Barron, Joseph, Male

Name on recommendation, 1804, by citizens of Knox County that General John Gibson be appointed Indian Agent.
Territorial Papers of the US - volume: 7 page: 251
Bass, Etho T, Indiana Territory Knox County
Bass, Etho T, Male
Name on recommendation, 1804, by citizens of Knox County that General John Gibson be appointed Indian Agent.
Territorial Papers of the US - volume: 7 page: 250
Beggs, Charles, Indiana Territory County, Vincennes
Beggs, Charles, Male
Name on recommendation, 28 Dec 1802, of John Rice Jones for judge of the territory who "has resided as a practising attorney in the said Territory for many years".
Territorial Papers of the US - volume: 7 page: 83
Bond, Shadrach, Indiana Territory County, Vincennes
Bond, Shadrach, Male
Name on recommendation, 28 Dec 1802, of John Rice Jones for judge of the territory who "has resided as a practising attorney in the said Territory for many years".
Territorial Papers of the US - volume: 7 page: 83
Bullitt, Benjn, Indiana Territory Knox County
Bullitt, Benjn, Male
Name on recommendation, 1804, by citizens of Knox County that General John Gibson be appointed Indian Agent.
Territorial Papers of the US - volume: 7 page: 251
Bullitt, Wm, Jr Indiana Territory Knox County
Bullitt, Wm, Jr Male
Name on recommendation, 1804, by citizens of Knox County that General John Gibson be appointed Indian Agent.
Territorial Papers of the US - volume: 7 page: 251
Carruthers, Wm, Indiana Territory Knox County
Carruthers, Wm, Male
Name on recommendation, 1804, by citizens of Knox County that General John Gibson be appointed Indian Agent.
Territorial Papers of the US - volume: 7 page: 251
Claypool, Jere., Indiana Territory Knox County

Claypool, Jere., Male
Name on recommendation, 1804, by citizens of Knox County that General John Gibson be appointed Indian Agent.
Territorial Papers of the US - volume: 7 page: 251
Claypoole, Go, Indiana Territory Knox County
Claypoole, Go, Male
Name on recommendation, 1804, by citizens of Knox County that General John Gibson be appointed Indian Agent.
Territorial Papers of the US - volume: 7 page: 251
Collins, William, Indiana Territory Knox County
Collins, William, Male
Name on recommendation, 1804, by citizens of Knox County that General John Gibson be appointed Indian Agent.
Territorial Papers of the US - volume: 7 page: 250
Davis, Tho. T, Indiana Territory Knox County
Davis, Tho. T, Male
Name on recommendation, 1804, by citizens of Knox County that General John Gibson be appointed Indian Agent.
Territorial Papers of the US - volume: 7 page: 251
Decker, Luke, Indiana Territory Knox County
Decker, Luke, Male
Name on recommendation, 1804, by citizens of Knox County that General John Gibson be appointed Indian Agent.
Territorial Papers of the US - volume: 7 page: 251
Decker, Luke, Indiana Territory County, Vincennes
Decker, Luke, Male
Name on recommendation, 28 Dec 1802, of John Rice Jones for judge of the territory who "has resided as a practising attorney in the said Territory for many years".
Territorial Papers of the US - volume: 7 page: 83
Dubois, , Indiana Territory Knox County
Dubois, , Male
Name on recommendation, 1804, by citizens of Knox County that General John Gibson be appointed Indian Agent.
Territorial Papers of the US - volume: 7 page: 251
Edwards, Andrew, Indiana Territory Knox County

Edwards, Andrew,   Male
Name on recommendation, 1804, by citizens of Knox County that General John Gibson be appointed Indian Agent.
Territorial Papers of the US - volume: 7 page: 251
Estes, Peter,   Indiana Territory   Knox County
Estes, Peter,   Male
Name on recommendation, 1804, by citizens of Knox County that General John Gibson be appointed Indian Agent.
Territorial Papers of the US - volume: 7 page: 251
Gibson, John, General Indiana   Territory
Knox County
Gibson, John, General   Male
He is the "Secretary to the Territory".
He is being recommended, 1804, by citizens of Knox County to be appointed Indian Agent [pages 249-251].
Territorial Papers of the US - volume: 7 page: 249
Gilmore, Robt, Senr   Indiana   Territory
Knox County
Gilmore, Robt, Senr   Male
Name on recommendation, 1804, by citizens of Knox County that General John Gibson be appointed Indian Agent.
Territorial Papers of the US - volume: 7 page: 251
Green, Cha B.,   Indiana   Territory
Knox County
Green, Cha B.,   Male
Name on recommendation, 1804, by citizens of Knox County that General John Gibson be appointed Indian Agent.
Territorial Papers of the US - volume: 7 page: 251
Harrison, Willm H.,   Indiana Territory
County, Vincennes
Harrison, Willm H.,   Male
Name on recommendation, 28 Dec 1802, of John Rice Jones for judge of the territory who "has resided as a practising attorney in the said Territory for many years".
Territorial Papers of the US - volume: 7 page: 83
Hurst, Henry, Indiana Territory   Knox County
Hurst, Henry,   Male
Name on recommendation, 1804, by citizens of Knox County that General John Gibson be appointed Indian Agent.
Territorial Papers of the US - volume: 7 page: 251

Johnson, Ja,   Indiana Territory   Knox County
Johnson, Ja,   Male
Name on recommendation, 1804, by citizens of Knox County that General John Gibson be appointed Indian Agent.
Territorial Papers of the US - volume: 7 page: 251
Johnson, Jno, Indiana Territory   Knox County
Johnson, Jno,   Male
Name on recommendation, 1804, by citizens of Knox County that General John Gibson be appointed Indian Agent.
Territorial Papers of the US - volume: 7 page: 251
Johnston, W., Genl   Indiana   Territory
Knox County
Johnston, W., Genl   Male
Name on recommendation, 1804, by citizens of Knox County that General John Gibson be appointed Indian Agent.
Territorial Papers of the US - volume: 7 page: 251
Johnston, Washington,   Territory NW of Ohio River   Knox County, Vincennes
Johnston, Washington, Male
"In 1783 emigrated from Virginia to Vincennes, in which town he was the first attorney admitted to practice; subsequently circuit judge and legislator in the State of Indiana"
Appointed Deputy Postmaster of Vincennes "on a former occasion".
Territorial Papers of the US - volume: 3 page: 78
Johnston, Washington, General   Indiana Territory
Johnston, Washington, General Male
"since his residence in this Country, which has been nearly Twelve Years during which time he has been in the Practice of the Law,"
Recommendation, 2 Dec 1807, to the President by residents of Indiana that he (General Washington Johnston) be appointed judge in place of Thomas T. Davis who passed away [pages 504-505].
Territorial Papers of the US - volume: 7 page: 504
Johnston, William,   Indiana   Territory
Knox County
Johnston, William,   Male
Name on recommendation, 1804, by citizens of Knox County that General John Gibson be appointed Indian Agent.
Territorial Papers of the US - volume: 7 page: 251

Jones, Jno Rice, Indiana Territory Knox County
Jones, Jno Rice, Male
Name on recommendation, 1804, by citizens of Knox County that General John Gibson be appointed Indian Agent.
Territorial Papers of the US - volume: 7 page: 251
Jones, Peter, Indiana Territory Knox County
Jones, Peter, Male
Name on recommendation, 1804, by citizens of Knox County that General John Gibson be appointed Indian Agent.
Territorial Papers of the US - volume: 7 page: 251
Jones, Rice, Indiana Territory Knox County
Jones, Rice, Male
Name on recommendation, 1804, by citizens of Knox County that General John Gibson be appointed Indian Agent.
Territorial Papers of the US - volume: 7 page: 251
Jordan, Ephm, Indiana Territory Knox County
Jordan, Ephm, Male
Name on recommendation, 1804, by citizens of Knox County that General John Gibson be appointed Indian Agent.
Territorial Papers of the US - volume: 7 page: 250
Kuykendall, Ja, Indiana Territory Knox County
Kuykendall, Ja, Male
Name on recommendation, 1804, by citizens of Knox County that General John Gibson be appointed Indian Agent.
Territorial Papers of the US - volume: 7 page: 251
Light, John, Indiana Territory Knox County
Light, John, Male
Name on recommendation, 1804, by citizens of Knox County that General John Gibson be appointed Indian Agent.
Territorial Papers of the US - volume: 7 page: 251
McConnell, Saml, Indiana Territory Knox County
McConnell, Saml, Male
Name on recommendation, 1804, by citizens of Knox County that General John Gibson be appointed Indian Agent.
Territorial Papers of the US - volume: 7 page: 251

McKee, Samuel, Jr Indiana Territory Knox County
McKee, Samuel, Jr Male
Name on recommendation, 1804, by citizens of Knox County that General John Gibson be appointed Indian Agent.
Territorial Papers of the US - volume: 7 page: 251
Menard, Pierre, Indiana Territory County, Vincennes
Menard, Pierre, Male
Name on recommendation, 28 Dec 1802, of John Rice Jones for judge of the territory who "has resided as a practising attorney in the said Territory for many years".
Territorial Papers of the US - volume: 7 page: 83
Mills, William, Indiana Territory Knox County
Mills, William, Male
Name on recommendation, 1804, by citizens of Knox County that General John Gibson be appointed Indian Agent.
Territorial Papers of the US - volume: 7 page: 251
Moredock, John, Indiana Territory County, Vincennes
Moredock, John, Male
Name on recommendation, 28 Dec 1802, of John Rice Jones for judge of the territory who "has resided as a practising attorney in the said Territory for many years".
Territorial Papers of the US - volume: 7 page: 83
Morrison, Robt, Indiana Territory County, Vincennes
Morrison, Robt, Male
Name on recommendation, 28 Dec 1802, of John Rice Jones for judge of the territory who "has resided as a practising attorney in the said Territory for many years".
Territorial Papers of the US - volume: 7 page: 83
Neal, James, Indiana Territory Knox County
Neal, James, Male
Name on recommendation, 1804, by citizens of Knox County that General John Gibson be appointed Indian Agent.
Territorial Papers of the US - volume: 7 page: 250
Onielle, Jh., Indiana Territory Knox County
Onielle, Jh., Male
Name on recommendation, 1804, by citizens of

Knox County that General John Gibson be appointed Indian Agent.
Territorial Papers of the US - volume: 7 page: 251
Perrey, , Indiana Territory County, Vincennes
Perrey, , Male
Name on recommendation, 28 Dec 1802, of John Rice Jones for judge of the territory who "has resided as a practising attorney in the said Territory for many years".
Territorial Papers of the US - volume: 7 page: 83
Phelon, Richd, Indiana Territory Knox County
Phelon, Richd, Male
Name on recommendation, 1804, by citizens of Knox County that General John Gibson be appointed Indian Agent.
Territorial Papers of the US - volume: 7 page: 251
Prince, Wm, Indiana Territory Knox County
Prince, Wm, Male
Name on recommendation, 1804, by citizens of Knox County that General John Gibson be appointed Indian Agent.
Territorial Papers of the US - volume: 7 page: 251
Prince, Wm, Indiana Territory County, Vincennes
Prince, Wm, Male
Name on recommendation, 28 Dec 1802, of John Rice Jones for judge of the territory who "has resided as a practising attorney in the said Territory for many years".
Territorial Papers of the US - volume: 7 page: 83
Purcell, Andrew, Indiana Territory Knox County
Purcell, Andrew, Male
Name on recommendation, 1804, by citizens of Knox County that General John Gibson be appointed Indian Agent.
Territorial Papers of the US - volume: 7 page: 251
Purcell, James, Indiana Territory Knox County
Purcell, James, Male
Name on recommendation, 1804, by citizens of Knox County that General John Gibson be appointed Indian Agent.
Territorial Papers of the US - volume: 7 page: 251
Purcell, John, Indiana Territory Knox County
Purcell, John, Male

Name on recommendation, 1804, by citizens of Knox County that General John Gibson be appointed Indian Agent.
Territorial Papers of the US - volume: 7 page: 251
Purcell, Jonathan, Indiana Territory Knox County
Purcell, Jonathan, Male
Name on recommendation, 1804, by citizens of Knox County that General John Gibson be appointed Indian Agent.
Territorial Papers of the US - volume: 7 page: 251
Purcell, Jonathan, Jur Indiana Territory Knox County
Purcell, Jonathan, Jur Male
Name on recommendation, 1804, by citizens of Knox County that General John Gibson be appointed Indian Agent.
Territorial Papers of the US - volume: 7 page: 251
Purcell, Noah, Indiana Territory Knox County
Purcell, Noah, Male
Name on recommendation, 1804, by citizens of Knox County that General John Gibson be appointed Indian Agent.
Territorial Papers of the US - volume: 7 page: 251
Purcell, William, Indiana Territory Knox County
Purcell, William, Male
Name on recommendation, 1804, by citizens of Knox County that General John Gibson be appointed Indian Agent.
Territorial Papers of the US - volume: 7 page: 251
Reynolds, Robt, Indiana Territory County, Vincennes
Reynolds, Robt, Male
Name on recommendation, 28 Dec 1802, of John Rice Jones for judge of the territory who "has resided as a practising attorney in the said Territory for many years".
Territorial Papers of the US - volume: 7 page: 83
Rizley, David, Indiana Territory Knox County
Rizley, David, Male
Name on recommendation, 1804, by citizens of Knox County that General John Gibson be appointed Indian Agent.
Territorial Papers of the US - volume: 7 page: 251
Rodamer, Jos., Indiana Territory Knox County
Rodamer, Jos., Male

Name on recommendation, 1804, by citizens of Knox County that General John Gibson be appointed Indian Agent.
Territorial Papers of the US - volume: 7 page: 251
Rose, Mathias, Indiana Territory Knox County
Rose, Mathias, Male
Name on recommendation, 1804, by citizens of Knox County that General John Gibson be appointed Indian Agent.
Territorial Papers of the US - volume: 7 page: 251
Scott, John, Indiana Territory Knox County
Scott, John, Male
Name on recommendation, 1804, by citizens of Knox County that General John Gibson be appointed Indian Agent.
Territorial Papers of the US - volume: 7 page: 251
Simpson, Patrick, Indiana Territory Knox County
Simpson, Patrick, Male
Name on recommendation, 1804, by citizens of Knox County that General John Gibson be appointed Indian Agent.
Territorial Papers of the US - volume: 7 page: 251
Smith, Daniel, Indiana Territory Knox County
Smith, Daniel, Male
Name on recommendation, 1804, by citizens of Knox County that General John Gibson be appointed Indian Agent.
Territorial Papers of the US - volume: 7 page: 251
Snyder, William, Indiana Territory Knox County
Snyder, William, Male
Name on recommendation, 1804, by citizens of Knox County that General John Gibson be appointed Indian Agent.
Territorial Papers of the US - volume: 7 page: 251
sturgus, Robt A, Indiana Territory Knox County
sturgus, Robt A, Male
Name on recommendation, 1804, by citizens of Knox County that General John Gibson be appointed Indian Agent.
Territorial Papers of the US - volume: 7 page: 251
Tingley, Benjamin, Indiana Territory Knox County
Tingley, Benjamin, Male

Name on recommendation, 1804, by citizens of Knox County that General John Gibson be appointed Indian Agent.
Territorial Papers of the US - volume: 7 page: 251
Vander Burgh, Henry, Indiana Territory Knox County
Vander Burgh, Henry, Male
Name on recommendation, 1804, by citizens of Knox County that General John Gibson be appointed Indian Agent.
Territorial Papers of the US - volume: 7 page: 251
Vigo, , Indiana Territory County, Vincennes
Vigo, , Male
Name on recommendation, 28 Dec 1802, of John Rice Jones for judge of the territory who "has resided as a practising attorney in the said Territory for many years".
Territorial Papers of the US - volume: 7 page: 83
Wallace, Geo., Junr Indiana Territory Knox County
Wallace, Geo., Junr Male
Name on recommendation, 1804, by citizens of Knox County that General John Gibson be appointed Indian Agent.
Territorial Papers of the US - volume: 7 page: 251
Weaver, James, Indiana Territory Knox County
Weaver, James, Male
Name on recommendation, 1804, by citizens of Knox County that General John Gibson be appointed Indian Agent.
Territorial Papers of the US - volume: 7 page: 251
Welton, Jonathan, Indiana Territory Knox County
Welton, Jonathan, Male
Name on recommendation, 1804, by citizens of Knox County that General John Gibson be appointed Indian Agent.
Territorial Papers of the US - volume: 7 page: 251
Westfall, Isaac, Indiana Territory Knox County
Westfall, Isaac, Male
Name on recommendation, 1804, by citizens of Knox County that General John Gibson be appointed Indian Agent.
Territorial Papers of the US - volume: 7 page: 251
Williams, Joseph, Indiana Territory Knox County
Williams, Joseph, Male

Name on recommendation, 1804, by citizens of Knox County that General John Gibson be appointed Indian Agent.
Territorial Papers of the US - volume: 7 page: 251
Williams, William, Indiana Territory
Knox County
Williams, William, Male
Name on recommendation, 1804, by citizens of Knox County that General John Gibson be appointed Indian Agent.
Territorial Papers of the US - volume: 7 page: 251
Woo[d], James N., Indiana Territory
County, Vincennes

Woo[d], James N., Male
Name on recommendation, 28 Dec 1802, of John Rice Jones for judge of the territory who "has resided as a practising attorney in the said Territory for many years".
Territorial Papers of the US - volume: 7 page: 83
Wyant, Christopher, Indiana Territory
Knox County
Wyant, Christopher, Male
Name on recommendation, 1804, by citizens of Knox County that General John Gibson be appointed Indian Agent.
Territorial Papers of the US - volume: 7 page: 251

STEMMONS PUBLISHING, 1078 Shields Lane, South Jordan, Utah 84095, 801-254-2152 (Call between 9:00 a.m. and 5:00 p.m. Monday through Friday. If no one answers, please leave a message.), stemmonspublishing@gmail.com

The importance of census records and other population lists cannot be overstated in terms of the help they are in locating people in a specific area. This allows one to examine other records in that area. This is one of our main goals and why we do business. What we are trying to accomplish is a work in progress. We hope to improve as we go along. Thank you for your patience.

Petitions are an important example of these population lists.

Thank you for the opportunity to serve you.

Sincerely,
John Stemmons

A COMPLETE LIST OF OUR GENEALOGY BOOKS

AL-01 **ALABAMA 1800 PETITIONERS [-1804]**© Compiled by John D Stemmons, 2021. This book compiled from *Territorial Papers of the United States* contains 253 entries for a very early period in Alabama's history. It may contain some biographical details and clues to prior residence. It can help substitute for the missing federal census. For information on how to obtain this book search by the title or "Books by John Stemmons" at Amazon.com. This comes automatically with a paperback binding. It includes but is not limited to petitions regarding:
- Seeking new territory due to the rapid migration from Georgia, etc.
- Petition seeking confirmation of land grants obtained from other governments.

36 Pages $7.20

AL-02 **ALABAMA 1810 PETITIONERS, ETC., [1805-1814]**© Compiled by John D Stemmons, 2021. This book compiled from *Territorial Papers of the United States* contains 1687 entries for a very early period in Alabama's history. It includes a census of Madison County, taken Jan 1809. It may contain some biographical details and clues to prior residence. It can help substitute for the missing federal census. For information on how to obtain this book search by the title or "Books by John Stemmons" at Amazon.com. This comes automatically with a paperback binding. It includes but is not limited to petitions regarding:
- Issues relating to land.
- Petition of inhabitants east of Pearl River seeking to form a new territory.
- 1809 census of Madison County.
- Inhabitants of Tombigbee seeking for their purchases from the Spanish to be duty free at "Fort Stoddart".

176 Pages $35.20

AL-03 **ALABAMA 1820 PETITIONERS, ETC., [1815-1824]**© Compiled by John D Stemmons, 2021. This book compiled from *Territorial Papers of the United States* contains 3913 entries for a fast-growing period in Alabama's history. It may contain some biographical details and clues to prior residence. It can help substitute for the missing federal census. For information on how to obtain this book search by the title or "Books by John Stemmons" at Amazon.com. This comes automatically with a paperback binding. It includes but is not limited to petitions regarding:
- Merchants and traders of St. Stephens seeking to establish that town as a port of delivery.

- Inhabitants of eastern part of MS territory, who lost much income/property in the wars with England & Indians.
- Inhabitants of Alabama Territory opposing the "settlements on the western side of the Mobile & Tombigby rivers" being made part of Mississippi.
- List of Letters, 9 Jan 1819, remaining in Huntsville Post Office.
- Issues about military and local officers.
- Memorial, ref. 20 Jan 1817, to Congress from inhabitants of Mobile complaining that Ft Charlotte is indefensible.

407 Pages $81.40

AR-01 ARKANSAS PETITIONERS, ETC. 1800, 1810 [1795-1814]© Compiled by John D Stemmons, 2021. This book compiled from *Territorial Papers of the United States* contains 261 entries and is a partial replacement for the missing federal censuses of 1800 and 1810. As a result, it is a very helpful resource in establishing residence of people in Arkansas during that early formative period in the state's history. These people include some of earliest you will find that established the foundation of what was to become the great state that Arkansas now is. This also makes it possible to determine what other records might be available for further research. Some additional biographical details may be included, and possible relationships with others may be revealed. For information on how to obtain this book search by the title or "Books by John Stemmons" at Amazon.com. This comes automatically with a paperback binding. It includes but is not limited to petitions regarding:
- Issues relating to land.
- Inhabitants of Arkansas District expressing concern about the hostile attitude of the Cherokees nearby.
- Issues about military and local officers.

43 Pages $8.60

AR-02 ARKANSAS PETITIONERS, ETC. 1820 [1815-1824]© Compiled by John D Stemmons, 2021. This book compiled from *Territorial Papers of the United States* contains 1936 entries and is a partial replacement for the missing federal census of 1820. As a result, it is a very helpful resource in establishing residence of people in Arkansas during that fast-growing territorial period prior to becoming a state. Unfortunately, the 1820 census is not available to help track these people. That is why this new book can help. It is even better in some respects than the census because it helps us understand some of the challenges they faced. It also makes possible the determination of other records that might be available for further research. Some additional biographical details may be included, and possible relationships with others may be revealed. Even the names of some Native Americans are included as well as a few potential residents of Oklahoma. For information on how to obtain this book search by the title or "Books by John Stemmons" at Amazon.com. This comes automatically with a paperback binding. It includes but is not limited to petitions regarding:
- Issues relating to land.
- Issues relating to Native Americans.
- Citizens of Arkansas County describing the good location of the Town of Arkansas.
- Appointments about military and local officers, etc.
- Inhabitants of Arkansas and Phillips Counties seeking a mail route from the Town of Arkansas to the "Post of Ouachita in Louisianna."
- Abstract of Grand and Petit Jurors, Oct term, 1824 listing compensation for their attendance at a Superior Court held at Little Rock.

216 Pages $43.20

1001-GEORGIA PETITIONS 1778-1784© Compiled by John D Stemmons, 2004. This book contains 256 entries for a very early period in Georgia's history. For information on how to obtain this book search by the title or "Books by John Stemmons" at Amazon.com. This comes automatically with a paperback binding. It includes but is not limited to petitions regarding:
- A desire for a new district.
- A request for local courts.
- Issues about military and local officers.
- Request for protection against enemies.
- A request for pardon, amnesty, etc.
- Description of hardship.

44 pages $8.80

1002-GEORGIA PETITIONS 1785-1794© Compiled by John D Stemmons, 2004. Contains 3720 entries which includes about 25% of the heads of household in Georgia at that time. As such this publication is an excellent substitute for the missing Georgia 1790 federal census. It even includes many names for Burke and Washington Counties which suffered severe record loss in the early years. For information on how to obtain this book search by the title or "Books by John Stemmons" at Amazon.com. This comes automatically with a paperback binding It includes but is not limited to petitions regarding:
- Issues regarding local agencies, boundary changes, etc.
- Issues regarding religion and churches.
- Issues about military and local officers.
- Asking for measures to control slaves.
- Recommendation for a business opportunity.
- Seeking resolution of land problems, land fraud, etc.
- Asking for increased tobacco inspection fees.
- Request for protection against Indians.
- Issues about crimes, pardon, amnesty, etc.
- Description of hardship.

367 pages $73.40

IL-01 ILLINOIS PETITIONS, ETC., 1760-1810 [1755-1814]© Compiled by John D Stemmons, 2021, this book contains 3680 names from *The Territorial Papers of the U.S.* This covers a period of time even before the federal census of 1790. And while no federal censuses exists for Illinois from 1790-1810, these records nicely substitute for those missing documents It should be noted that **1004-A PARTIAL CENSUS FOR INDIANA TERRITORY 1810** includes most if not all the names for 1810. A study to determine that they were the same was inconclusive and so, just in the outside chance there might be some that were not the same, it was felt that they should be included. The convenience of having them together outweighs their exclusion. These records include an incredible amount of information about these early people. One can see the change from a mostly French culture to that of English. The transition was not always peaceful. Included are census records, lists of inhabitants, and much more. While the federal censuses are missing that would help track these people, these records are even better in some respects than the census because it helps us understand some of the challenges they faced. That is why this new book can help. Some additional biographical details may be included, plus possible relationships with other family members. For information on how to obtain this book search by the title or "Books by John Stemmons" at Amazon.com. This comes automatically with a paperback binding. It includes but is not limited to petitions regarding:
- Issues relating to land.
- Issues relating to Native Americans.
- List of inhabitants at Kaskaskias before 1783.
- Appointments about military and local officers, etc.
- Lands claimed and possessed by inhabitants of the District of Cahokia on or before 1783 that still existed after 29 May 1790.
- Applications for lands in the District of Cahokia by persons claiming as settlers under the state of Virginia, if the settlements were made on or before 1783 that still existed after 29 May 1790.
- List of families at the Prairie du Pont, undated, but enclosed in St. Clair's report 10 Feb 1791.

349 Pages $69.80

IN-01 THE TERRITORY NORTHWEST OF THE RIVER OHIO, PETITIONERS, ETC., 1790-1800 [1785-1804] (Present day Indiana)© Compiled by John D Stemmons, 2021. This book was compiled from *Territorial Papers of the United States*. 1790 contains 242 names found on petitions, etc., including a census of heads of household for Vincennes. 1800 only includes 76 names and so is not as valuable as 1790. The population of Indiana would have increased significantly between 1790 and 1800. This is still a very early time prior to Indiana becoming a state. Unfortunately, there is no 1790 or 1800 census existing to help track these people. Therefore, we must do what we can with what is available. That is why this new book is so helpful. It is even better in some respects than the census because it helps us understand some of the challenges they faced. It also makes possible the determination of other records that might be available for further research such as land grants. Even the names of some Native Americans are listed. Some additional biographical details may be included, plus possible relationships with other family members. For information on how to obtain this book search by the title or "Books by John Stemmons" at Amazon.com. This comes automatically with a paperback binding. It includes but is not limited to petitions regarding:

- Issues relating to land.
- Heads of families settled at Post Vincennes on or before 1783 and residents at this time [13 Jul 1790] who are entitled to donation lands.
- Issues relating to Native Americans.
- Inhabitants of Vincennes who migrated to Vincennes around 1786 and received land, but never obtained a deed.
- Appointments about military and local officers, etc.

38 Pages $7.60

1003-INDIANA ELECTION RETURNS 1809, 1812© Compiled by John D and E. Diane Stemmons, 2004. This compilation of 3576 entries includes the names found in the territorial election returns which documents are in the Indiana Historical Society. Also included is a poll book of an election for Dearborn County in 1809 as found in *Territorial Papers of the United States*. All entries in this book are also found in *A Partial Census for Indiana Territory 1810*. The book *Indiana Election Returns, 1809, 1812* was compiled for just the election returns simply because they are one entire record source and may have some value in that. For information on how to obtain this book search by the title or "Books by John Stemmons" at Amazon.com. This comes automatically with a paperback binding.

285 pages $57.00

1004-A PARTIAL CENSUS FOR INDIANA TERRITORY 1810© Compiled by John D and E. Diane Stemmons, 2021. With 8602 entries this book includes name lists found in *Territorial Papers of the United States* for Indiana Territory during the period 1805 through 1814. It also provides the names in *Indiana Election Returns 1809, 1812* listed above. Since there were approximately 4300 heads of households in the territory in 1810, *A Partial Census for Indiana Territory 1810* probably lists virtually every head of household in Indiana Territory for the time period. It makes an excellent substitute for the missing federal census for 1810. In addition, it includes names of people living in what is now Illinois, but which was part of Indiana Territory before 1809. Therefore, *A Partial Census for Indiana Territory 1810* is also a partial census of Illinois in the years between 1805 to 1809. For information on how to obtain this book search by the title or "Books by John Stemmons" at Amazon.com. This comes automatically with a paperback binding. It includes but is not limited to petitions regarding:

- Issues relating to land.
- Heads of families settled at Post Vincennes on or before 1783 and residents at this time [13 Jul 1790] who are entitled to donation lands.
- Issues relating to Native Americans.

- Inhabitants of Vincennes who migrated to Vincennes around 1786 and received land, but never obtained a deed.
- Appointments about military and local officers, etc.

574 pages $114.80

KY-01 KENTUCKY 1800, BARREN COUNTY TAX BOOK© Compiled by John D Stemmons, 2021. It contains 494 names from the Barren County tax list and 1 from *The Territorial Papers of the U.S.* Even though the 1800 census is missing this list it provides an amazing amount of information that substitutes nicely for that missing census, including white and black males aged 16-21 and those 21 and over. This is the kind of information one would expect to find on the census for that period. This list includes all taxable heads of household. Some additional biographical details may be included, plus possible relationships with other family members. The names of the blacks may be found in court, land, and probate records. For information on how to obtain this book search by the title or "Books by John Stemmons" at Amazon.com. This comes automatically with a paperback binding.

65 Pages $13.00

LA-01 ARKANSAS PETITIONS 1800 [1795-1804] and ORLEANS TERRITORY (NOW LOUISIANA) PETITIONS, ETC., 1800 [1795-1804]© Compiled by John D Stemmons, 2021. This book was compiled from *Territorial Papers of the United States* and contains 495 names for Louisiana and 3 from Arkansas. Since no federal census exists for Arkansas and Louisiana for 1800, these records nicely substitute for those missing documents. These records include an incredible amount of information about these early people. While the federal censuses are missing that would help track these people, these records are even better in some respects than the census because it helps us understand some of the challenges they faced. That is why this new book can help. Some additional biographical details may be included, plus possible relationships with other family members. For information on how to obtain this book search by the title or "Books by John Stemmons" at Amazon.com. This comes automatically with a paperback binding. It includes but is not limited to petitions regarding:

- Inhabitants of Pointe Coupee to Gov. Claiborne, requesting military aid because of fears of a slave revolt.
- Characterization of New Orleans residents, 1 July 1804.
- Address from the free people of color Jan. 1804, volunteering for military service.
- Memorial to Congress from merchants of New Orleans, 9 Jan 1804, offering allegiance to the US.
- Appointments about military and local officers, etc.

47 Pages $9.40

MO-01 MISSOURI PETITIONERS, ETC., 1780-1820 [1775-1824]© Compiled by John D Stemmons, 2021. This book was compiled from *Territorial Papers of the United States* and contains 1 name for 1780, 12 names for 1790, 19 names for 1800, 5057 names for 1810, and 1509 names for 1820. The later lists begin to approach the number needed to include most heads of household, and nicely substitute for missing or no censuses. These records include an incredible amount of information about these early people. While censuses help track people, the records this book includes are even better in some respects than the census because it helps us understand some of their personal feelings and challenges, they faced. Some additional biographical details may be included, plus possible relationships with other family members. For information on how to obtain this book search by the title or "Books by John Stemmons" at Amazon.com. This comes automatically with a paperback binding. It includes but is not limited to petitions, etc., regarding:

- Resolution recommending distinction between Americans and Frenchmen should be done away.
- Letter from U.S. President to Chief White Hairs and the

warriors of the Osages, informing them of the Lewis and Clark expedition, and promising them a resident agent.

- Many petitions, etc., expressing their support and confidence in Governor Wilkinson. He was involved in scandals and controversies.
- Memorial recommending replacements for Governor Wilkinson.
- Petition expressing concern about changing the form of territorial government before they are adequately prepared.
- Memorial concerning the large number of their Spanish land claims that are being rejected.
- Lists of civil and military officers.
- Petition seeking a grant of a township of land for the support of the school as had been done in other areas.
- Petition seeking pre-emption rights for the services given in defending the frontier in Boon's Lick Settlement around 1815.
- Petitions relating to the New Madrid & Little Prairie earthquake.
- Petitions asking for new post offices and routes, etc.

552 pages $110.40

MI-01 **MICHIGAN PETITIONS, ETC. 1790-1810 [1785-1814]**©

Compiled by John D Stemmons, 2021. This book was compiled from *Territorial Papers of the United States*. It contains 1 name for 1790, 794 names for 1800, and 1335 names for 1810. Clearly, that is not enough for 1790, but the others begin to approach the number needed. Especially is this so for 1810 because we are fortunate enough to have much of what appears to be the federal 1810 census. Since no federal census exists for 1800, these records nicely substitute for those missing documents. These records include an incredible amount of information about these early people. While censuses help track people, the records this book includes are even better in some respects than the census because it helps us understand some of their personal feelings and challenges, they faced. Some additional biographical details may be included, plus possible relationships with other family members. For information on how to obtain this book search by the title or "Books by John Stemmons" at Amazon.com. This comes automatically with a paperback binding. It includes but is not limited to petitions regarding:

- Inhabitants of Detroit seeking new territory because of distance to travel to the headquarters of Indiana Territory.
- Appointments about military and local officers, etc.
- Inhabitants of Wayne County seeking clarification of the status of their land.
- 1810 Census of the District of Detroit.
- Inhabitants of Michigan Ter. seeking time to file claims to their land.
- List, 23 Jul 1812, of patents received from the General Land Office for private claims in the District of Detroit.
- Petition from inhabitants of Michigan Territory asking that the new territorial code be printed also in French.
- Petition to Thomas Jefferson, from inhabitants of Michigan Territory complaining of Governor William Hull and Supreme Court Chief Justice Augustus B. Woodward.

222 Pages $44.40

MS-01 **MISSISSIPPI TERRITORIAL PETITIONERS, ETC. 1800 [1795-1804]**©

Compiled by John D Stemmons, 2021. This book was compiled from *Territorial Papers of the United States and* contains 2566 names found on petitions, etc., from Mississippi Territory for this time period. This was during a fast-growing era prior to Mississippi becoming a state. Unfortunately, there is no 1800 census existing to help track these people. That is why this new book can help. It is even better in some respects than the census because it helps us understand some of the challenges they faced. It also makes possible the determination of other records that might be available for further research such as Spanish land grants. Some additional biographical details may be included, plus possible relationships with other family members. For information on how to obtain this book search by the title or "Books by John Stemmons" at Amazon.com. This comes automatically with a paperback binding. It includes but is not limited to petitions regarding:

- Citizens of territory asking land office to be in the area, settlers have pre-emption right, & suffrage be for males of age and US citizens & residents of territory for 6 months.
- Memorial by citizens of the territory, who obtained land before the area became part of the US.
- Testimonials ca 1802, by individuals regarding the service of John Steele, secretary of the territory.
- Memorial by citizens of the territory seeking that "moderate grants [be] made to actual settlers on unappropriated lands,"
- Merchants of Natchez, complaining of the extra duties they must pay for merchandise shipped from the US.

209 Pages $41.80

MS-02 **MISSISSIPPI TERRITORIAL PETITIONS, ETC. 1810 [1805-1814] and WEST FLORIDA 1820 PETITIONERS [1815-1824]**©

Compiled by John D Stemmons, 2021. This book was compiled from *Territorial Papers of the United States* and contains 1061 names found on petitions, etc., from Mississippi Territory for the period 1810 [1805-1814]. It also includes a list of 76 names on a petition to Congress, 11 Dec 1816, by inhabitants of Jackson County, Mississippi Territory, many of whom settled on land in West Florida while under Spanish control and now seek for their grant to be confirmed by the US. It is being included with Mississippi Territory because it is basically the same time period and place of residence. This was during a fast-growing time prior to Mississippi and Florida becoming states. Unfortunately, there is no 1810 or 1820 census existing to help track these people. That is why this new book can help. It is even better in some respects than the census because it helps us understand some of the challenges they faced. It also makes possible the determination of other records that might be available for further research. Some additional biographical details may be included, and possible relationships with others may be revealed. For information on how to obtain this book search by the title or "Books by John Stemmons" at Amazon.com. This comes automatically with a paperback binding. It includes but is not limited to petitions regarding:

- Inhabitants of the territory seeking adjustment of land claims obtained from the British Government.
- Inhabitants of the territory seek for a road to be built that follows the Pearl River which would shorten the route from Nashville to New Orleans.
- Inhabitants of Amite and Wilkinson Counties seek establishment of a post office.
- Memorial by citizens of the territory (Americans by birth?) seeking a postponement of statehood for the territory.
- Inhabitants of Jackson Co. Mississippi Territory, many of whom settled on land in West Florida while under Spanish control seek for their grant to be confirmed by the US.

108 Pages $21.60

NJ-01-**NEW JERSEY PETITIONS 1740, 1745 THROUGH 1754**©

Compiled by John D Stemmons, 2021. It contains 740 entries for a period of time in New Jersey when records are sparse. While that may not seem like very many names, it was during the time when the population was small, and the residence of people was sometimes hard to track. In looking through these petitions, it appears that the people of this era had basically the same concerns we have. One can see the forces of democracy beginning to stir that were to result in independence from Great Britain just a short three decades away. We can obtain a hint of the personal concerns of these people and what was important to them in this exciting historical time. Even at this time of great distress and hardship life had to go on. These petitions are almost like an open window into the lives of these people. For information on how to obtain this book search by the title or "Books by John Stemmons" at Amazon.com. This comes automatically with a paperback binding. It includes but is not limited to petitions regarding:

- Issues regarding exports and imports.
- Issues regarding devaluation of currency, money supply, etc.
- Issues regarding local agencies, boundary changes, etc.
- Seeking new legislation.
- Issues about military and government officers.
- Seeking resolution of land problems, etc.
- Protesting against the great number of taverns.
- Resolution of tax issues.
- Issues about crimes, pardon, amnesty, etc.

84 pages $16.80

NJ-02-NEW JERSEY PETITIONS 1755-1764© Compiled by John D Stemmons, 2004. Contains 2389 entries from many petitions submitted because of concerns about the French and Indian War. This book is an excellent census substitute. For information on how to obtain this book search by the title or "Books by John Stemmons" at Amazon.com. This comes automatically with a paperback binding. It includes petitions regarding:

- Issues regarding local agencies, boundary changes, etc.
- Issues about roads, bridges, etc.
- Opposition to importing slaves.
- Seeking naturalization.
- Seeking new legislation.
- Issues about military and government affairs.
- Request for reimbursement from the government.
- Request for protection against enemies.
- Seeking resolution of land problems, etc.
- Protesting against dispensing of "spirituous liquors"
- Issues about crimes, pardon, amnesty, etc.
- Description of hardship.

246 pages $49.20

NJ-03-NEW JERSEY PETITIONS 1765-1774© Compiled by John D Stemmons, 2004. This book contains 806 entries. While a small percent of the population, it represents the time leading up to the Revolution. For information on how to obtain this book search by the title or "Books by John Stemmons" at Amazon.com. This comes automatically with a paperback binding. It includes but is not limited to petitions regarding:

- Issues regarding agriculture, exports and imports.
- Request for permission to beg, financial support, etc.
- Issues about religion and churches.
- Request for medical standards.
- Issues regarding devaluation of currency, money supply, etc.
- Issues regarding local agencies, boundary changes, etc.
- Issues on hunting, fishing, etc.
- Issues about roads, bridges, etc.
- Issues relating to slavery.
- Issues about military and government affairs.
- Seeking resolution of land problems, etc.
- Issues about crimes, pardon, amnesty, etc.

99 pages $19.80

NJ-04-NEW JERSEY PETITIONS 1775-1784© Compiled by John D Stemmons, 2005. This book contains 6201 entries which is about 29% of the heads of household living in New Jersey at that time (not counting duplicate names.) It represents the historic period during the Revolution. For information on how to obtain this book search by the title or "Books by John Stemmons" at Amazon.com. This comes automatically with a paperback binding. It includes but is not limited to petitions regarding:

- Issues regarding trade, exports, and imports.
- Issues regarding devaluation of currency, money supply, price controls, etc.
- Issues on religion and churches.
- Issues regarding local agencies, boundary changes or disputes, etc.
- Issues on court cases.
- Request for guardianship of children.
- Issues about roads, bridges, canals, etc.
- Issues on slavery.
- Seeking new legislation or repealing old laws.
- Issues about military and government affairs and officers.
- Issues about payment from the government.
- Issues on independence and the Revolutionary War.
- Request for protection against enemies.
- Seeking resolution of property and land problems, etc.
- Issues about crimes, pardon, amnesty, etc.
- Resolution of tax issues.

559 pages $111.80

NJ-05-NEW JERSEY PETITIONS 1785-1794 Volumes 1-2© Compiled by John D Stemmons, 2005. This book contains 10,353 entries which covers about 35% of the heads of household for that time, not counting duplicate names. For information on how to obtain this book search by the title or "Books by John Stemmons" at Amazon.com. This comes automatically with a paperback binding. It includes but is not limited to petitions regarding:

- Economic issues regarding the devaluation of currency, public debt, etc.
- Issues on religion and churches.
- Issues regarding counties and towns, etc.
- Issues on court cases.
- Issues regarding hunting on private property, fishing, etc.
- Issues about roads, bridges, canals, ferries, etc.
- Issues relating to schools.
- Issues on slavery.
- Seeking new legislation or repealing existing laws.
- Issues about military and government affairs and officers.
- Seeking payment from the government.
- Expressing approval of the U.S. Constitution.
- Seeking resolution of property and land problems, etc.
- Issues about crimes, pardon, amnesty, etc.
- Resolution of tax issues.

Volume 1, A Through K, pages 462 $92.40
Volume 2, L Through Z, pages 470 $94.00

NJ-06 NEW JERSEY PETITIONERS, ETC., 1800 [1795-1804] Volumes 1-3© Compiled by John Stemmons, 2021. All volumes of this book contain 13,144 names. Unlike the tax ratables, these records cover the entire state for the period just after the Revolutionary War These records provide a place of residence which can lead to other records to search. For information on how to obtain this book search by the title or "Books by John Stemmons" at Amazon.com. This comes automatically with a paperback binding. It includes but is not limited to petitions regarding:

- Public buildings including poor house, taverns, banks, etc.
- Issues on religion and churches.
- Issues regarding counties and towns, etc.
- Issues on court cases.
- Concerning voting opportunities
- Issues about roads, bridges, canals, ferries, water rights, storage of gunpowder, etc.
- Issues relating to schools.
- Issues on slavery.
- Seeking new legislation or repealing existing laws.
- Issues about military and government affairs and officers.

- Seeking payment from the government.
- Seeking resolution of property and land problems, etc.
- Issues about crimes, pardon, amnesty, etc.
- Resolution of tax issues.

Volume 1, A Through E, pages 423	$84.60
Volume 2, F Through R, pages 529	$105.80
Volume 3, S Through Z, pages 358	$71.60

NJ-07 NEW JERSEY TAX RATABLES, 1770 [1765-1774] This book contains 2373 names of those who are taxable. They do include important details about the property they held and may provide clues regarding relationship, etc. For information on how to obtain this book search by the title or "Books by John Stemmons" at Amazon.com. This comes automatically with a paperback binding.
250 pages　　　　　　　　　　$50.00

NJ-08 NEW JERSEY TAX RATABLES, 1780 [1775-1784] This book contains 4358 names of those who are taxable. It includes important details about the property they held and may provide clues regarding relationship, etc. For information on how to obtain this book search by the title or "Books by John Stemmons" at Amazon.com. This comes automatically with a paperback binding.
440 pages　　　　　　　　　　$88.00

NJ-09 NEW JERSEY TAX RATABLES, 1790 [1785-1794] This book contains 2307 names of those who are taxable. Unfortunately, Burlington and Cape May counties are not covered by this period. We are fortunate though in have the petitions that cover the same time. It is interesting to compare the two sets of records. They were not combined because that would make the books too large. The tax ratables do include important details about the property they held and may provide clues regarding relationship, etc. For information on how to obtain this book search by the title or "Books by John Stemmons" at Amazon.com. This comes automatically with a paperback binding.
268 pages　　　　　　　　　　$53.60

NJ-10 NEW JERSEY TAX RATABLES, 1800 [1795-1804] , Volumes 1-2 This book contains 8396 names of those who are taxable. It includes important details about the property they held and may provide clues regarding relationship, etc. For information on how to obtain this book search by the title or "Books by John Stemmons" at Amazon.com. This comes automatically with a paperback binding.

Volume 1, A Through K, pages 456	$91.20
Volume 2, L Through Z, pages 449	$89.80

NC-01 NORTH CAROLINA PETITIONERS, ETC. 1780 [1775-1784]© Compiled by John Stemmons, 2021. This book contains 4866 names and was assembled from records located at the North Carolina State Archives. This was before the federal census was taken and is a valuable resource for locating people in this early time. Included are some names from what is now, Tennessee. For information on how to obtain this book search by the title or "Books by John Stemmons" at Amazon.com. This comes automatically with a paperback binding.

- Economic issues regarding the devaluation of currency, public debt, etc.
- Issues on religion and churches.
- Issues regarding counties and towns, etc.
- Issues regarding hunting on private property, fishing, etc.
- Issues about roads, bridges, canals, ferries, etc.
- Seeking new legislation or repealing existing laws.
- Issues about military and government affairs and officers.
- Seeking resolution of property and land problems, etc.
- Issues about crimes, pardon, amnesty, etc.

568 pages　　　　　　　　　　$113.60

1009-ROWAN COUNTY, NORTH CAROLINA TAX LISTS 1758/1759, 1761, 1768, 1778, 1779© Compiled by John D and E. Diane Stemmons, 2004. This publication serves as a census for Rowan County for about three decades which includes two major conflicts, the French and Indian and Revolutionary wars. Thus, one may be able to track individuals that stayed in the county over a significant period of time. Sometimes sons and slaves are given plus other important information. These tax lists are listed alphabetically in three separate sections.
218 pages　　　　　　　　　　$43.60

OH-01 TERRITORY NW OF OHIO RIVER, PETITIONERS, ETC. 1790-1800 [1785-1804] (Now Ohio)© Compiled by John D Stemmons, 2021. It contains 217 names for 1790 and 3047 names for 1800. This book may include many heads of household at that time and serves as a substitute for missing or no censuses. It even incorporates the names of many native Americans. These records provide an incredible amount of information about these early people. While censuses help track people, the records this book contains are even better in some respects than the census because it helps us understand some of their personal information not recorded by a census. Some additional biographical details may be included, plus possible relationships with other family members. For information on how to obtain this book search by the title or "Books by John Stemmons" at Amazon.com. This comes automatically with a paperback binding. It includes but is not limited to petitions regarding:

- Petition of the French inhabitants of Gallipolis regarding their purchase of lands from the Scioto Company.
- Inhabitants on the Muskingum to Governor St. Clair.
- Petitions about land and issues with John Cleves Symmes.
- 1800, Population Schedules. Washington County. Territory Northwest of the River Ohio.
- Petition by inhabitants telling of losses in the "Late Indian war" and their inability to obtain land in Kentucky.
- Petition by inhabitants of Hamilton County seeking approval to purchase reserved land in order to build a grist mill because it has a sufficient stream of water.
- List of Gallipolis proprietors and the amount of their land purchases.

285 pages　　　　　　　　　　$57.00

PA-01 PENNSYLVANIA CHESTER COUNTY TAX LIST 1771© Compiled by John D Stemmons, 2021. It contains 5621 names. This record lists all taxable people in the county, and as such, is a good census substitute. It is not known what is meant by the abbreviations or "inmate". Perhaps they were incarcerated in jail or were indentured in some way. Often an occupation is listed. Occasionally there will be information about family relationships. It is helpful that this book includes the information about the taxable property. For information on how to obtain this book search by the title or "Books by John Stemmons" at Amazon.com. This comes automatically with a paperback binding.
399 pages　　　　　　　　　　$79.80

South Carolina

South Carolina has a remarkable series of records that makes it unique for the Colonial period. These are the "Jury Lists" compiled by the government to function as a list of names from which members of a jury could be assigned. They cover the period 1720-1783 and, according to the act in 1731, were compiled from tax lists of the preceding year [which no longer exist], listing every person who paid a tax of twenty shillings or more. Those who paid five pounds or more were listed as grand jurors. The poorer class of people would not be listed. While not a complete list of the heads of household, they represent a sizeable proportion. They serve as a census during a period of growth, migration, and war. Usually only the name is given, but sometimes an occupation or name of the father is listed, etc. Many names are on more than one list for a particular year.

1010-SOUTH CAROLINA 1720 JURY LIST© Compiled by John D and E. Diane Stemmons, 2004. This publication has 840 entries covering a time when South Carolina was only 50 years old and the

population was very small with only an estimated 885 heads of household. Unfortunately, it does not list a residence other than South Carolina. For information on how to obtain this book search by the title or "Books by John Stemmons" at Amazon.com. This comes automatically with a paperback binding.
48 pages $9.60

1017-SOUTH CAROLINA 1731 JURY LIST© Compiled by John D and E. Diane Stemmons, 2005. This book contains 2160 entries. It lists the locality of every person. For information on how to obtain this book search by the title or "Books by John Stemmons" at Amazon.com. This comes automatically with a paperback binding.
110 pages $22.00

1011-SOUTH CAROLINA 1740 JURY LIST© Compiled by John D and E. Diane Stemmons, 2004. This book contains 2160 entries. It lists the locality of every person. For information on how to obtain this book search by the title or "Books by John Stemmons" at Amazon.com. This comes automatically we a paperback binding.
111 pages $22.20

1012-SOUTH CAROLINA 1751 JURY LIST© Compiled by John D and E. Diane Stemmons, 2004. This book contains 2170 entries. It lists the locality of every person. For information on how to obtain this book search by the title or "Books by John Stemmons" at Amazon.com. This comes automatically with a paperback binding.
109 pages $21.80

1013-SOUTH CAROLINA 1757 JURY LIST© Compiled by John D and E. Diane Stemmons, 2004. This book contains 2624 entries. It lists the locality of every person. For information on how to obtain this book search by the title or "Books by John Stemmons" at Amazon.com. This comes automatically with a paperback binding.
135 pages $27.00

1014-SOUTH CAROLINA 1767 JURY LIST© Compiled by John D and E. Diane Stemmons, 2004. This book contains 2385 entries. It lists the locality of every person. For information on how to obtain this book search by the title or "Books by John Stemmons" at Amazon.com. This comes automatically with a paperback binding.
127 pages $25.40

SC-07 SOUTH CAROLINA 1780 [1775-1784], VOLUMES 1-2© Compiled by John D Stemmons, 2021. It contains 13,444 names. This record of jury lists consist of many people during the Colonial/Revolutionary War period and as such, is a good census substitute. Since Loyalists owned property that they paid taxes on, they may be included as well. These records provide a place of residence which can lead to other records to search. For information on how to obtain this book search by the title or "Books by John Stemmons" at Amazon.com. This comes automatically with a paperback binding.
Volume 1, 502 pages $100.40
Volume 2, 575 pages $115.00

TN-01 TENNESSEE PETITIONS, ETC., 1770-1790 [1765-1794]© Also known as Territory South of Ohio River. Compiled by John Stemmons, 2021. This book was assembled from *Territorial Papers of the United States* and contains 1 name for 1770, 12 names for 1780, and 1161 names for 1790. These people listed seem to be the more prominent persons, so, most of the less noteworthy individuals would not be listed. Still, the people listed clarify this early time before Tennessee became a state. The amount of biographical information is significant compared to the other books we have compiled from *Territorial Papers of the United States*. Many Native American names are included. For information on how to obtain this book search by the title or "Books by John Stemmons" at Amazon.com. This comes automatically with a paperback binding. It includes but is not limited to petitions regarding:

- "One of twelve men selected by the Cumberland people to govern the settlement, 1783; appointed by the Governor of North Carolina judge of the courts, Davidson County, 1783.
- Appointments about military and local officers, etc.
- Name on the "Treaty of Holston", 2 Jul 1791 between the President of the US and "Chiefs and Warriors of the Cherokee Nation of Indians."
- Memorial, 1 Aug 1791, to the President from the civil and military officers of Mero District explaining recent depredations of the Indians and seeking an "Act of Cession" from North Carolina.
95 pages $19.00

TN-02 TENNESSEE PETITIONERS, ETC. AND GRAINGER COUNTY TAX LISTS 1800 [1795-1804]© Compiled by John Stemmons, 2021. Also known as Territory South of Ohio River. This book was assembled from Grainger County Tax Lists 1800 and *Territorial Papers of the United States* and contains 182 names for the *Papers* and 247 names for the tax lists. From *Territorial Papers of the United States* the names mostly seem to be persons appointed to official or military positions or are members of the Knoxville Convention. Thus, they seem to be the more prominent persons, so, most of the less noteworthy individuals would not be listed. Still, the people listed clarify this early time before Tennessee became a state. The tax lists record the names of those who are taxable and are much more inclusive. They do include important details about the property they held. For information on how to obtain this book search by the title or "Books by John Stemmons" at Amazon.com. This comes automatically with a paperback binding. It includes but is not limited to petitions regarding:

- List, 21 Dec 1795, of members of Knoxville Convention.
- Appointments of military and local officers, etc.
49 pages $9.80

TN-03 TENNESSEE GRAINGER COUNTY TAX LISTS 1810 [1805-1814]© Compiled by John Stemmons, 2021. This book was assembled from Grainger County Tax Lists 1810 and contains 1242 names of those who are taxable. They do include important details about the property they held and may provide clues regarding relationship, etc. For information on how to obtain this book search by the title or "Books by John Stemmons" at Amazon.com. This comes automatically with a paperback binding.
146 pages $29.20

TN-04 TENNESSEE GRAINGER COUNTY TAX LISTS 1820 [1815-1824]© Compiled by John Stemmons, 2021. This book was assembled from Grainger County Tax Lists 1820 and contains 1161 names of those who are taxable. They do include important details about the property they held and may provide clues regarding relationship, etc. The lists for 1800-1820 furnish an excellent opportunity to track the population growth of the county. For information on how to obtain this book search by the title or "Books by John Stemmons" at Amazon.com. This comes automatically with a paperback binding.
131 pages $26.20

VA-01 VIRGINIA PERSONAL PROPERTY TAX LISTS, 1780 [1775-1784] (Accomack and Albemarle Counties)© Compiled by John Stemmons, 2021. This book was assembled from Accomack and Albemarle Counties Personal Property Tax Lists ca 1780 and contains 2553 names of those who are taxable. They do include important details about the property they held and may provide clues regarding relationship, etc. They even furnish the entry for, it is assumed, future president Thomas Jefferson! For information on how to obtain this book search by the title or "Books by John Stemmons" at Amazon.com. This comes automatically with a paperback binding.
252 pages $50.40

VA-02 VIRGINIA PERSONAL PROPERTY TAX LISTS, 1790 [1785-1794] (Accomack and Albemarle Counties)© Compiled by John Stemmons, 2021. This book was assembled from Accomack and Albemarle Counties Personal Property Tax Lists ca 1790 and contains 2679 names of those who are taxable, plus 3 from *Territorial Papers of the U.S.* They do include important details about the property they held and may provide clues regarding relationship, etc. They even furnish the entry for, it is assumed, future president Thomas Jefferson! Data on the age range of males is also included. For information on how to obtain this book search by the title or "Books by John Stemmons" at Amazon.com. This comes automatically with a paperback binding.

333 pages $66.60

VA-03 VIRGINIA PERSONAL PROPERTY TAX LISTS, ca 1800 [1795-1804] (Accomack and Albemarle Counties)© Compiled by John Stemmons, 2021. This book was assembled from Accomack and Albemarle Counties Personal Property Tax Lists ca 1800 and contains 3788 names of those who are taxable. They do include important details about the property they held and may provide clues regarding relationship, etc. They even furnish the entry for, it is assumed, future president Thomas Jefferson! Data on the age range of males is also included. With the lists for 1780-1800 one can track population growth in these countries. An individual showing up for the first time may indicate potential age. For information on how to obtain this book search by the title or "Books by John Stemmons" at Amazon.com. This comes automatically with a paperback binding.

436 pages $87.20

Population estimates were obtained from U.S. Bureau of the Census, *Historical Statistics of the United States, Colonial Times to 1957,* Washington, D.C., 1960, Library of Congress Card No. A 60-9150; and United States. Bureau of the Census, *A Century of Population Growth From the First Census of the United States to the Twelfth, 1790-1900* Washington: Government Printing Office, 1909. A household size of 5.7 persons was assumed.

Good morning.

We received the gift book of "Georgia Petitions 1785-1794". Fantastic book and a great tool in researching that time period. I like the format which is easy to read and puts in one place the petitions for research. I personally have searched many of the petitions and love this new tool. The introduction and the list of petitions gives much added information to understanding the petitions for the various individuals.

I look forward to ordering more books in July after our budget is in place. Thank you for contacting our library and making us aware of your fine publications. Have a great day.

Thanks,

Irene Godwin

Ellen Payne Odom Genealogy Library

204 5th St. S.E.

P.O. Box 2828

Moultrie, GA 31768

EXAMPLES OF THE KIND OF INFORMATION CONTAINED IN OUR BOOKS

Cicotte, J. Bte.,   Michigan Territory, District of Detroit, "Cote des Poux"

Cicotte, J. Bte.,	45-Over?	Male	**Color:**	White	
10-16		Male	**Color:**	White	
10-16		Male	**Color:**	White	
16-26		Male	**Color:**	White	
45-Over		Female	**Color:**	White	

1810 Census of the District of Detroit

MS/Witherell (B. F. H.) Collection, LMS, Burton Historical Collection, Detroit Public Library, Folder 2

Cicotte, Jacques,   Michigan Territory

      Cicotte, Jacques,   Male

Petition, 26 Oct 1807, to Congress from inhabitants of Michigan Ter. seeking time to file claims to their land, claims on 1+ parcels be confirmed, farms on Detroit River be extended to 80 arpents, & occupancy later than 1 Jul 1796 be allowed [pp. 138-49].

Territorial Papers of the US - volume: 10 page: 146

Holeday, Jas,   Territory NW of Ohio River   Knox County, Vincennes

      Holeday, Jas,   Male

Address to Colonel Josiah Harmar by American inhabitants of Post Vincennes dated 4 Aug 1787

Territorial Papers of US - volume: 2 page: 65

Holliday, Heirs of James,   Territory NW of Ohio River   Knox County, Vincennes

      Holliday, Heirs of James,   Male

Petition, 7 Aug 1797, to Congress by inhabitants of Knox County, who migrated to Vincennes around 1786 and received land, but never obtained a deed.

Territorial Papers of US - volume: 2 page: 621

Lajoye, Pierre ,   Spanish North America, St. Louis

      Lajoye, Pierre,   Male

      "Pierre Lajoye, formerly of Prairie du Rocher on the American side of the Mississippi".

Letter, 1790, by Governor St. Clair to Manuel Perez concerning an American boy in the possession of Pierre Lajoye [pages 237-238].

"Mr. Mayet has just complained to me that a Mr. La Joye, to whom he has entrusted an American boy, whom he took from the savages, to be returned to the parents of the latter, has not returned him, but is holding the boy as a slave and refuses to return the boy to them on the pretext of some debt. I am convinced that you will not find it proper that a free child should be held as a slave for the debts of another--and will order Mr. La Joye to return him to Mayet."

Letter, 26 May 1790, from St. Louis by Manuel Perez to Governor St. Clair concerning an American boy in the possession of Pierre Lajoye [pages 237-240]:

"MY DEAR SIR: In order to take cognizance of the subject of the claim in your favor of the 20th instant concerning the child who is today in the possession of Mr. Lajoye, I had the latter appear before me and from the questions which I put to him and the reasons which he advanced to me

35

on this subject I have found in him only a disposition to render service to the Unhappy Father who lost him and who asks for him in a letter of which the said Mr. Lajoye is the bearer.

After studying this matter carefully, I find that the above-mentioned child claimed by Mr. Mayet can leave the possession of Mr. Lajoye only to go to that of the Father now living at Natches. I think also that it is just for the said Mr. Mayet to be reimbursed for what he actually gave the savages in order to get him out of their barbarous hands; . . .

When the young man arrived at Mr. Lajoye's house, he came and notified me of it at once and that he would write to the lower part of the Colony to learn in what district the Father of the said child lived. He learned later from the letter of which he is the bearer, that he resides at Natchez; accordingly he will send him down on the first opportunity."

Territorial Papers of the US - volume: 2 page: 237

Mayfield, Geddeon, Kentucky Barren County

      Mayfield, Geddeon, Male

Acres of land: 200; Barren Co.; watercourse: Mill Creek; Entry: Geddeon Mayfield; Survey: same; Patent: 0; white males over 21: 0; white males 16-21: 0; blacks over 16: 0; total blacks: 0; horses: 0; stud horses: 0; retail stores: 0; tavern license: 0.

Barren County Tax Book, 1800, part 1 - page: 10 FAMILY HISTORY LIBRARY film 7865

LEGISLATIVE PETITIONS

Petitions to the governor, legislature, etc., were a particularly important way for individuals to communicate with their government regarding issues that were very essential to them. Their influence in making changes throughout our history has contributed to making our society what it is today. They are an important link in our legislative and judicial history. In these early petitions one can trace the growing desire for democracy. In fact, they are one of the most visible manifestations of democracy in practice. It is fascinating to view the changes in the reasons for submitting petitions over time (see the lists below.)

Because petitions represent the feelings of one or more individuals, they provide a window into the soul of the petitioners that illuminates the historical landscape. Most aspects of the human condition are addressed in some form by these important documents. The names listed with the petition can be used as a census of inhabitants for a particular locality. Often it is possible to determine useful information about individual persons from these records. They can help compensate for lost or destroyed county records. Petitions are original records that contain historical background about our culture and society.

Unfortunately, petitions are among the most inaccessible and underused records because there are so many, they are often difficult and time-consuming to read, and are usually housed only in the state archives or other repository in their un-microfilmed condition.

To help resolve this problem, we have abstracted the content of many petitions and indexed the names of the petitioners. A brief context of the petition is provided with each name. Generally, we have not included those petitions with fewer than 10-12 names.

GENEALOGY AND LOCAL HISTORY BOOKS IN PDF FORMAT ON A FLASH DRIVE

705 Local and Family History books for $75-or 11 cents a book!!! All 4 volumes of Savage's Genealogical Dictionary of New England would cost you about $0.44!*

You can have in your library/home more books of this type than most libraries have. They cover nearly all aspects of human experience including law, medicine, biography, history, etc., etc.

Concerns?

1. **Question:** I am uncomfortable in letting patrons use this small drive as it may become lost.

Answer: Simply download the contents of the drive onto your computer(s) and keep the drive in a safe place. We will replace it at no charge if it becomes lost.

2. **Question:** Some of our books, including those on microfilm, that are also on your flash drive are in poor condition because of patron use through the years, especially when copies are made. Copies made from microfilm are not always the best quality. How can you help us with these problems?

Answer: Once our books are on your computers, your originals can be kept in a secured area so that no more damage will occur because of hands-on use. The images on the computer can be easily printed, usually with better quality.

3. **Question:** We are only interested in items covering the locality our patrons live in.

Answer: Many of your patrons were born outside of your area and/or have ancestry from all over the United States, etc.

4. **Question:** Are these books under copyright restrictions?

Answer: They are in the public domain and so are not copyrightable.

Approximately how many pages do the 705 books add up to?
Total cost (from Stemmons Publishing) for hard copies: $7044 (not available now)
Approximated total pages of text on the flash drive: 221,307
Approximated total images on the flash drive: 58,272

A huge genealogical library of 705 books on your computer for only $75
A dealer's discount is available of $45 for 5 or more flash drives.
Imagine 705 books… 60,417 images… 230,642 pages on a small flash drive.

You may be able to find these books on Google, Ancestry, or FamilySearch. To make a hard copy from these sources may be expensive, especially if you were to copy all 705! I may be mistaken, but I'm not sure you can print just a single page from those services. You can with my books. You also have them immediately at your fingertips without needing to go to the effort to search these other services.
The downside to these books is that many are not indexed.
No problem: just check the index provided by these other sources before using our books.
"In 2016, popular genealogy blogger Dick Eastman surmised that perhaps ninety percent of the resources you may need to fill out your family tree are not yet available on the Internet." This statement was found on the Boston Public Library website. If that is true, some of the books on our flash drive may not be found on the Internet.

You may obtain a copy of the drive by sending check, money order, or cash to John Stemmons at 1078 Shields Lane, South Jordan, Utah, 801-254-2152 (Call between 9:00 a.m. and 5:00 p.m. Monday through Friday. If no one answers, please leave a message.), stemmonspublishing@gmail.com. We have been in this business since 1975! Check BBB if you need to.

The fee for shipping and handling is $10.00 unless you send a shipping container, deliverable to you, with sufficient postage to mail to you. Please allow 4-6 weeks for delivery.

The books on the drive are in the public domain and are not copyrighted. You may make as many copies of them as you would like. Please do not place the contents of the drive, in part or in full, on the Internet except for individual pages.

We do not do credit cards and PayPal. If you are unhappy with the drive, please return it for a refund of your money.

If you would like a list of questions and answers or a list of the books, please let us know.

*How are we able to do this? Simply by reducing each page so that 2-6 pages can be placed on a single 8½ by 11 sheet of paper and still be readable. With the computer, you can enlarge it as many times as needed.

Number of books by locality:
US-99, Regional-32, AL-1, CT-31, DE-1, GA-2, IL-1, IN-1, KY-1, ME-23, MD-15, MA-91, MI-1, MN-1, MO-2, NH-20, NJ-28, NY-81, NC-9, OH-9, PA-51, RI-6, SC-26, VT-2, VA-47, WV-1; Family History-62; CN-5; EN-39; IR-10; SCOT-7=705 books!